The Inventurers

The Inventurers
Excursions in Life
and Career Renewal

Janet Hagberg • Richard Leider

Addison-Wesley Publishing Company, Inc.

Reading, Massachusetts • Menlo Park, California • New York
Don Mills, Ontario • Wokingham, England • Amsterdam • Bonn • Sydney
Singapore • Tokyo • Madrid • Bogotá • Santiago • San Juan

Library of Congress Cataloging in Publication Data

Hagberg, Janet.
   The inventurers.

   Bibliography: p.
   1. Self-actualization (Psychology) 2. Adulthood.
3. Personality and occupation. I. Leider, Richard.
II. Title.
BF637.S4H33 1982   158'.1   82–11333
ISBN 0–201–12790–3

Ninth Printing, July 1987

Portions of this book are adapted with permission from a 3M Company copyrighted program
developed by Human Renewal, Inc.

Copyright © 1982, 1978 by Addison-Wesley Publishing Company, Inc.

ISBN 0–201–12790–3
IJ-AL-8987

Contents

"The
Longest Journey
Starts with
Just One Step"

Tao Te Ching

Preface

The Inventurers is "just one step" to help you explore new directions—new options in your life and career. We have all thought about taking a step to explore our lifestyle or career dreams. For some of you, life already is a constant discovery of new options. Some of you probably think of your own business enterprise as an avenue to happiness. Others, perhaps satisfied with your career, will explore new leisure pursuits as an opportunity for fulfillment. Still others of you dream of an escape from it all—from the constraints, politics, or career impasses. Yet despite dreams, wishful thinking, and even plans, few people actually take "just one step" toward exploring their dreams. Why is this? Is there a special type of person who is inclined to step forward? Do special characteristics or conditions stimulate the process of life and career renewal? The answers to these questions are the heart of this book.

There is an old adage that *"there is only one way to eat an elephant—one bite at a time!"* Taking that first bite, or the first step, is what *The Inventurers* is all about. This book shares a life and career-renewal process designed to help you find out, step by step, what you want out of your life and career, then expand and explore your options. The key word is *process*. You will learn a process that you can use now, in six weeks, or in two years for developing your own practical system of life and career renewal. The process in this book has grown out of life and career-renewal experiences with a wide range of adult groups in business and industry, education, and government.

The words "life" and "career renewal" deserve some explanation. You will see these words often in this book. When those separate words are put together as "life and career renewal," the phrase means *the "process" of pe-*

riodically reassessing your lifestyle and work style in order to reflect and focus on new options which might make you more satisfied.

The word "career" in our society often connotes a demanding, rigorous, preordained life pattern to whose goals everything else is ruthlessly subordinated. In contrast, the word "career" in this book connotes meaningful and stimulating activity (paid or unpaid) whose goals include excitement, challenge, and social satisfactions.

This book is designed as a practical tool for you to use in your own life and career-renewal experiences. It should be a personal book, since each of your experiences will be uniquely yours. The tools help you plan, shape, and map your life and career options. Like any tools, they can be used skillfully or clumsily; they can be unused or misused. The way you use these tools depends on your preferred style. Different people learn in different ways. Before you start the process, you may want to review the ways others have used it:

- Read through the entire book systematically, stopping to do the exercises at the appropriate spots along the way. Complete one section (or chapter) at a time, taking time out to reflect and to write down your insights.

- Scan the book to get an overall understanding of the process. You can get an overview of the entire book in an hour or less. Then go back and do the exercises or read the chapters that seem appropriate.

- Read the book with a friend, spouse, or coworker. Discuss the exercises, comparing your responses and insights, or tape your responses and share the tapes.

- Read the book as part of a course, project, or structured learning effort. If a structured class is not available, create your own! Set up timetables and systematic ways to share your experiences with the group.

There is a story of a man who set a speed record for hiking the Appalachian Trail. Upon completion, he observed that he would like to do it over again—but this time at his leisure because he hadn't seen anything! A key to this renewal process is complete information and experience gathering, and that often takes time and reflection. There is no great rush to get to the end. Take your time and enjoy every step of this unique process. T. S. Eliot sums it up: *"We shall not cease from exploration and the end of all our exploring will be to arrive where we started and to know the place for the first time."*

This book is based on several assumptions about people. The process in the book reflects these assumptions:

1. *Coping with change:* We all have different styles of coping with "present shock"—the accelerating change around us. Some of us ignore it, others try to stop it, some of us run from it, and others try to change along with it. You need to learn what your style is and how to use it effectively.

2. *Untapped abilities:* Psychologist William James said that "95 percent of us live on 5 percent of our potential." You possess much untapped potential that could change your life considerably.

3. *Self-direction:* The basic ingredient in life and career renewal is *choice*—the choice of taking responsibility for yourself. In any situation, you have basically two options: change the situation or change the mind set that is perceiving the situation. The choice is yours alone. Many of us are more comfortable allowing others to make the choices, until we really experience the way that self-direction mobilizes us with enthusiasm and ingenuity.

4. *Organized planning:* Effectively assessing life and career-renewal options requires more than new insights and simple glimpses of the obvious. Your reflections must be organized and focused into an action plan in order to contribute to satisfying progress. And self-discipline is a virtue. We may have a wealth of planning skills, but seldom use them for our personal lives. If you put your planning skills to work with a process that is practical, you will be sure to make progress.

5. *Risk taking:* Choices involve risks. Risk is the element in career or life everyone wishes would go away. The idea that a life or career can be planned, predictable, and risk-free is, of course, not reality. The inventuring process emphasizes a balance between the need to plan and realize goals and the need to spontaneously live life as it unfolds.

AND NOW WE OFFER YOU THAT FIRST STEP!

Minneapolis, Minnesota   J. H.
March 1978   R. L.

Second Edition Preface

Since we wrote this book five years ago we have learned a lot about ourselves, about life, and about work. We have experienced our own life changes and career renewal and we have proceeded on the next stages of the *inventurers* path. There are a few reflections we would humbly offer in retrospect as we enter into the second edition of this book. They are, in our opinion. "excruciatingly simple":

- Although you start out asking one question, often you end up answering another.
- Being quiet is perhaps one of the finest means to self-knowledge there is.
- The longer we pursue them, life and career renewal not only become clearer, but also more of a mystery to us.
- The renewal process is never over.
- Although we talk about being in charge, taking responsibility, and inventuring, it is also imperative at some point that we then let go, give up control, and try not to get in the way of our life's purpose.
- Just when we think we know, we don't.

Minneapolis, Minnesota
February 1982

J.H.
R.L.

Acknowledgments

The inventuring model has been a fascinating one to see unfold. From the beginning it seemed to have an energy and an urgency of its own. Bits and pieces continue to emerge in the decade or so of our advising and consulting with organizations and individuals dealing with career renewal and change.

We are grateful to the people whose lives we observed over the years in order to write this book, the hundreds of people whose real experiences are reflected in these pages. We are also thankful for colleagues in the career development field and other fields who have inspired us, challenged us, and supported us. We would especially like to acknowledge Richard Bolles, whose *What Color Is Your Parachute?* led the way for us all. We also applaud two people who have gone far beyond the call of duty to encourage our continuing work in this field, and to whom we turn for support daily, our spouses, Dianne Leider and William Svrluga, Jr.

The Life
Inventure

I

The Inventurers

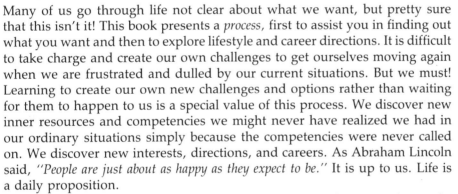

1

Many of us go through life not clear about what we want, but pretty sure that this isn't it! This book presents a *process*, first to assist you in finding out what you want and then to explore lifestyle and career directions. It is difficult to take charge and create our own challenges to get ourselves moving again when we are frustrated and dulled by our current situations. But we must! Learning to create our own new challenges and options rather than waiting for them to happen to us is a special value of this process. We discover new inner resources and competencies we might never have realized we had in our ordinary situations simply because the competencies were never called on. We discover new interests, directions, and careers. As Abraham Lincoln said, *"People are just about as happy as they expect to be."* It is up to us. Life is a daily proposition.

The expectations with which we start each morning determine the results we achieve. Life can produce fulfillment and happiness. Every day offers "the inventurer" an opportunity to see some aspect of life in a novel way. "What's an inventurer?" "What does inventuring mean?" *Webster's Dictionary* does not list these words. You will find *adventuring*—"to venture or to take a risk; as adventuring upon paths unknown." Well, inventurer and inventuring are new words.

AN INVENTURER:

You are an "inventurer" if you are one of those special breed of people who are taking charge and creating your own challenges to get yourself moving. More specifically, you are an inventurer if you are willing to take a long look at yourself and consider new options, venture inward, and explore. You are an inventurer if you see life as a series of changes, changes as growth experiences, and growth as positive. You are inventuring on life's *excursions* and learning about yourself as a result. You may feel lonely at times, and get discouraged for a while. But you are willing to risk some disappointments and take some knocks in your quest because you are committed to a balanced lifestyle and to more than just making a living. You are part of a unique group of people who want to make a living work. If you have these qualities, you are an inventurer.

Inventurers are people who choose to take a fresh look in the mirror to renew and perhaps recycle their lifestyles and careers. Some inventurers, seemingly snug in life and career patterns, are exploring their "greener pastures" or "South Seas island" dreams in search of their own personal Declaration of Independence: the pursuit of happiness. Other inventurers are planning second careers or early retirements. Some are underemployed and seeking careers more integrated with their abilities and lifestyles. They are female and male, old and young, and in between. Let's meet several of them:

John, age thirty-nine, slipped into his renewal. Everything had gone well for him. As director of marketing for a large bank, he "had it made." He got along well with his wife and his nine- and twelve-year-old children. In spite of all this, he began to feel vaguely uneasy. He was moody and depressed. His physical appearance was no longer acceptable to him. He grew a moustache, let his hair grow longer, and switched to more "mod" clothing styles. Then he became interested in women in his company who were much younger and had a brief affair with a trainee seventeen years his junior. He began to question everything, including the meaning of life itself. His days swung from periods of intense elation to sinking depressions. He pictured himself sliding quietly into old age and death. He still didn't know what he wanted to do when he grew up! He talked with a friend who recommended that he talk to a life and career-renewal specialist. What could it hurt? After a while, he began to see that his feelings were shared by many people. He started exploring lifestyle and career options. He discovered some interests and fantasies that had been wrapped up and stored away in his mind: "What happened to the kid who used to like to read and write short stories?" He developed a positive strategy and game plan. He enrolled as a part-time student in a creative writing lab to further his writing skills. He's looking for a small-town newspaper to buy. Together, he and his wife have developed new lifestyle interests and plan to move to a home with more outdoor space and privacy for John to write. Although he stayed with his current job, he has a new perspective on his career because his life has some direction. His job is no longer his sole identity.

Anne and Jim were climbing the tenure ladder in the anthropology department of a major university and feeling all the pressures to teach, publish, and attend meetings. They liked their work, but were beginning to get caught up in the bureaucracy. One particularly discouraging day, they asked themselves, "Are we going to let ourselves get caught in this forever?" A resounding "No!" So they got to thinking. What are we good at, and what do we really like to do? The answer was observing cultures and helping people reflect on their values. They decided to explore ways to use these skills in other work environments. After talking, thinking, and exploring with friends and community contacts for several months, they ended up participating as consultants on an interdisciplinary team exploring and reporting on the corporate culture of a local firm. They interviewed employees, fed back the data, and helped design ongoing programs to respond to employee needs. That project opened many other doors and they are now like new people, more excited than ever about their university work and able to see the connection to other work settings.

Twenty-four-year-old Barbara was a recent business school graduate. Her interests were quite broad, ranging from chamber music to oceanography. She graduated with honors and was offered jobs in a number of large firms. Her peers were accepting similar offers and questioning her reluctance to follow suit. Her father, a prominent New York executive, was encouraging her to try Wall Street. Her main concern was the whole question of lifestyle. She liked aspects of both a metropolitan and a rural setting. "I vacillate between Wall Street and a little book shop on the California coast." A career in oceanography would logically put her near the sea, which she loved. It would also satisfy her preference for a clean, outdoor lifestyle. But she had just finished her course work, and, given her upbringing, she had always had the ambition to test herself in a business situation. Maybe she should just try it for a few years. She thought it through and hesitatingly passed up the job offers to move to a California coastal town. She applied and was accepted into an excellent school of oceanography in a nearby university community. She's now working as the marketing director for a small manufacturing company, trying out the skills she learned in business school. She's happy she took the risk. She's living an integrated lifestyle, and that was her major priority.

These inventurers prove what the wise teachers have said for ages: *"The knowledge is right in us—all we have to do is clear our minds and open ourselves to see the obvious."*

"If I had my druthers . . ."

Stop for a moment— dream a little! Suppose money was no object and you could do anything or become anyone you chose. What would you do? Where?

12/11/88: I would be a politically active marine biologist, spending my work hours at sea with marine mammals and off hours helping develop global consciousness.
or
wildlife biologist managing a mountainous ecosystem.

In your search for career/life direction, we'd like to encourage you to dream, to fantasize about the kind of life and career you would like in your future. John Holland, a well-known vocational psychologist, has said that what you most wish to be is the most reliable prediction of your future vocational choice.

The hiker (or backpacker) is an applicable analogy to the inventurer. Inexperienced hikers soon learn the basic, if startling, assumption that they don't know how to walk. It isn't just a matter of putting one foot down in front of the other. There are techniques for hiking (even for resting) which create a more enjoyable experience. Inventurers, too, have techniques which help them cover many miles—and enjoy every one. Those techniques make up the process in this book.

There are several reasons for the ever-increasing popularity of the inventuring experience. First, like the hiker on the open road, the romantic spirit of the inventurer lurks in the psyche of every human being. Second, the hiker, on reaching the summit of a distant mountain, and the inventurer, on setting and reaching a goal, have a feeling of happiness and fulfillment. Third, the hiker has a sense of liberation by escaping the tension and hustle of daily life. The inventurer who discovers more balance in life feels a similar liberation.

Inventuring rekindles the sense of wonder and renewal, the exhilaration of a new challenge. Inventuring, however, is intended to be a pleasure and not an endurance test. Just as experienced hikers, eager to reach their destination, think nothing of hiking fifteen miles a day while toting a thirty-pound pack, an experienced inventurer thinks nothing of embarking on a new learning experience while holding a full-time job, because of the eagerness to discover new interests, directions, and careers.

Hikers plan or map their excursions. They select side trips, check overnight accommodations, tune up their equipment, and start packing. Inventurers extend these same considerations to their own lives. The excursion process in this book contains a special map. It looks exactly like the map in

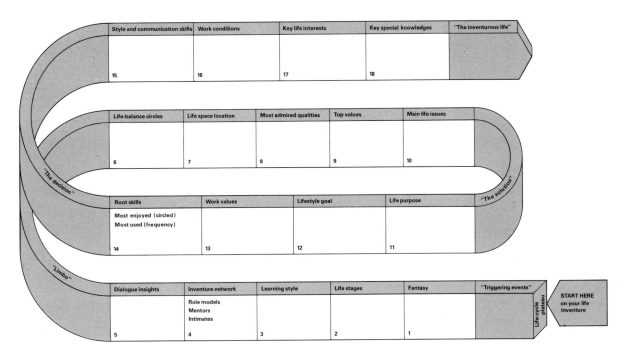

Figure 1.1. The excursion map.

fig. 1.1. Turn to your fold-out excursion map at the back of the book. This map will serve as a continuing itinerary as you read the book. At the end of exercises and chapters, you will be asked to go to your excursion map and log important insights. The foot symbol will signal you to turn to your map. When you complete the book, your map will provide a summary of the routes you have created toward new destinations. Start now by writing on your map key words from the fantasy you just completed (Box 1).

Whether or not you use a map depends on your preferred mode of travel— your style. The excursion map assists you in charting your own route; it helps you get out of the rut of accepting the usual paths or the tried-and-true trails and helps you to begin to discover your own creative routes.

Prepare yourself! We mean to send the blood flowing through your arteries and veins until you are tingling with newly discovered excitement about your options. For inventurers are agents of disturbance. They jog themselves out of their complacency and routines, their ruts. As someone once said, *"The only difference between a rut and a grave is the depth of the excavation!"* Inventurers prefer neither.

Inventurers—alive, aware, and excited about their lives—are in short supply. For every one who summons up the courage and determination to inventure, there are many more who hesitate, who are afraid, who plod on, waiting for some special moment, for a push up the hill! Often these "shelf-sitters" simply permit their lives to happen without mapping any direction. Or they make the mistake of trying to live their lives by what somebody else thinks they should be doing, instead of choosing the direction most rewarding to them personally. They seem to subscribe to the old adage, *"If you don't know where you're going, any road will probably get you there."*

The Postponed Life

2

We live in an age of exploration and adventure. We have reached the moon. Yet it is obvious that the real need for exploration and adventure resides in inner, rather than outer, space.

We are staggered by the rate of accelerating change. Future shock has become "present shock." The rules of the game change constantly. Turn on your television or pick up today's newspaper. "Present shock" leaves some of us immobilized—in a state of suspended animation! With so much change and stimulus competing for our attention, we often wonder which way to turn. Often the best we can do is to hold our ground and hang on, as the fiddler on the roof proposes, "just trying to maintain our balance."

"Present shock" affects some of us in the opposite way, and we run off in several directions at once, hoping that by trying several approaches to our problems, we might hit on *the* panacea or solution—*the* right mate, *the* right house, *the* right job, *the* right amount of money—to come our way and make us happy. Often we become postponers, waiting for *the* solution. In our waiting, we do experience some successful moments. But since we haven't mapped out what we're looking for to begin with, each magic solution gradually deteriorates.

In our quest for lifestyle and career solutions, we find that each option satisfies some needs and frustrates others. We are urged to change, but no one has told us how to change or how to map our way through the change.

Underlying this phenomenon is a fundamental truth: It is the thought patterns and expectations in our heads that make us unhappy, not the people and conditions outside ourselves (where we usually place the blame!). We have learned to live according to arbitrary expectations set up by the people and conditions in our lives (the infamous "they") rather than growing according to our own expectations. Further, in our desire to keep up with external expectations, we respond to every new stimulus, trying to keep up with a "they" that doesn't seem to know where "they" are going either. We become so skillful at being *reactive* to "they" that we forget how to be *proactive* in terms of "me."

If you are trying to adapt to external demands rather than discovering your own internal choices, you are setting yourself up as a slave. In fact, if "they" control your expectations and choices, then "they" should be the ones reading this book for you. Inventurers refuse to accept the slave role. They refuse to postpone their lives because of what "they" might think.

Inventurers refuse to live the up-and-down, hour-by-hour "postponed life" that "they" often seduce us to live:

- Wait until I find the right job (mate, house, etc.)—then . . .
- Wait until I get to be a manager (partner, president, etc.)—then . . .
- Wait until I have enough money (salary, savings, etc.)—then . . .
- Wait until the kids are through college, the mortgage paid—then . . .
- Wait until I retire—then . . .

THEN "I'LL START LIVING THE WAY *I* WANT TO, AND I'LL BE HAPPY!

Seconds accumulate into minutes, and the sequence unfolds through hours, days, weeks, months, and years to form the patterns of our lives. As the song by Harry Chapin goes, ". . . *there's no tick-tock on your electric clock, but still your life runs down.*" Year by year, the postponed life continues until we have a whole postponing society looking for new postponement quests as elusive as finding pots of gold at the end of the rainbow.

We fail to discover that we have 168 hours to live each week—no more, no less. For a thirty-four-year-old with an average life expectancy of seventy-four years, that equals 349,440 hours. Under normal habit patterns, those 349,440 hours look like this:

Sleep	116,480	33%
Work (commuting included)	174,720	50
Maintenance	30,000	11
Free time	28,240	6
	349,440	100%

Just a matter of time! How many hours do *you* expect to live? How do you spend your precious time?

Assuring ourselves that everyone around us also seems to be suffering from "postponement battle fatigue," we lower our expectations and decide that our form of happiness is probably not realistic anyway. We lower ourselves into our ruts—the postponed life is deadly!

This raises some curious questions: Why haven't we seriously challenged these patterns? Why is the postponed life so seductive? Why do we expect only small dribbles of happiness? Why do we map out only safe excursions (if we map at all)? It seems that either we're not aware, or we don't know how!

You *do* have options. You *can* choose to take control of your life and design strategies to begin living your life as a player rather than as a spectator. Instead of following someone else's map or fumbling around with no map at all, you can learn the skills to make change work for you creatively, one step at a time. To do this, you need to perceive clearly who you are and exactly what are the *real* conditions of your life. To achieve this clear perception takes steady work on these key questions:

1. Who am I?
2. Who is in control of my life?
3. What kind of lifestyle or balance in my life would make me happiest?
4. What skills and abilities do I have and most enjoy using?
5. Where and to what purpose do I want to use my most-enjoyed skills?
6. What options (or possibilities) fit my wants?
7. What holds me back from making changes?
8. How do I go about locating or creating situations for the options I choose?

The excursion process in this book helps you answer these questions. As a process, it is new, but many of the components have been tried and tested for thousands of years. These are old, old questions which are asked and answered in every era. Yet they are questions which all of us must ask and answer for ourselves in our own way. You have probably noted the amazing sources of energy available to people who have dealt with these questions, people who have a map. The world stands aside for a person with a plan!

Clearly, inventuring poses risks. But choosing not to inventure in an age of "present shock" may also be risky. Quite a few people who do not want to be pulled in a new direction now in a few years may find themselves pushed in one. Our fear of failure often keeps us from risking. There is usually no learning without some fumbling and failure. It's as simple as that! Life's too short for you not to be an inventurer. Marcus Aurelius (121–180 A.D.) wrote, "[People] *seek out retreats for themselves in the country, by the seaside, on the mountains, and thou too art wont to long above all for such things. But nowhere can a [person] find a retreat more full of peace than one's own soul. Make use then of this retirement continually and regenerate thyself."*

The Inventurous Life

3

Wake up! Or be awakened hastily by the events around you. It's time to choose to map your own excursion. Awakening to the "inventurous life," we often realize that we have been asleep—postponing life or perhaps calculating it rather than living it! Asleep, we did not understand what life is all about. We were not aware that the only real problem in our lives involves how consciously we are using our minds. Asleep, our lives were random patterns of events to be avoided. We did not realize that we were asleep; we did not see how life could be any different, did not understand that our sleep is not a metaphor, but real. Asleep, we believed that life should live up to our expectations, should be "this way" or "that way." Asleep, we drifted off into postponement: "When I get it all together in the future, then I'll start living, but until then. . . ." All of a sudden, we wake up to find that, as Sam Levinson states, *"When I finally got the means to an end, they moved the ends further apart."*

Inventurers have discovered the secret—the inventurous life. Inventurers know the difference between assuming personal responsibility for their every action, thought, feeling, or situation and assuming that they are caught up in actions over which they have no control. Is the difference exciting?

Jack is a fifty-four-year-old college biology professor. His awareness that he had arrived at a kind of plateau began when his son patted the back of his head and said, "Dad, you're getting bald." It was not just aging. After five decades of clearing the academic hurdles, learning to teach, learning what it meant to be married, he realized that an era of his life was over. His feelings were imprecise: "How shall I spend the balance of my life?" Feeling too comfortable with his current challenges, he mentioned his dilemma to his department head. To his astonishment, he received an intense negative reaction. "Was my willingness to disclose my uncertainties so threatening to him that he could only react by attacking me? How could anybody as fortunate as I am have questions about my life? What is wrong with me?" Nothing, of course. Jack came to understand that the feelings he thought were unique to him were, in fact, universal. He formed a support group in the university community for other staff people who were struggling with aspects of the fifty + dilemma. He published several articles in this area and gave several speeches to local business groups. His reputation spread. He developed a course on adult development with a colleague from the psychology department. He found that he had uncovered a strong need in his community. He applied for and received a fellowship to study adult-counseling practices. He has now returned to the university and has a half-time teaching appointment. With the other half of his time, he's opened a counseling practice. He's so excited that he can hardly wait to get up every morning!

Sooner or later it happens to most of us. We seek the inventurous life. As Sam Keen observes, *"We wake up one morning, the tide is out, and nothing is visible except mud flats."* The excitement of living has sunk! We go through the day postponing life, more like spectators than players.

The condition is common. James Thurber's word "slish" sounds like the way it feels—somewhere between slush and ish! The postponed life has become the common cold of the psyche. The combination of too many options, too much advice, and no guidelines turns normal change into a crisis. When we feel overwhelmed with life, we define it as a crisis. We postpone!

Psychologist John Brantner cites the following quote as a guide to living:

> *When we are depressed or discouraged*
> *or anxious,*
> *When we are embarrassed or*
> *ashamed,*
> *When we are taken by surprise*
> *These are the three surest signs*
> *That we are in a situation*
> *That offers the opportunity*
> *for growth.*
>
> (Anonymous)

Life is an upward spiral—a series of excursions—highs and lows. Anyone can handle the high points. The big moments take care of themselves. It's the valleys and plateaus, the postponements, that we must learn to handle. Nothing could be more normal than these plateaus and valleys; they are inevitable parts of human existence. But what is not normal is the way in which we cope with them.

Most of us realize that a crisis, dealt with successfully, creates growth and increases our sense of self-esteem. But what we do not know is how to meet crises (or perhaps even create them) in a positive way.

We cannot begin to make real changes in our lives—begin to work toward the happiness that is our birthright—until we begin to understand crises as a key to growth. Crises often herald a new stage of growth! Consider:

Writers: Eugene O'Neill and Joseph Conrad

Artists: Paul Gauguin and Goya

Architects: Frank Lloyd Wright and Charles Luckman

Visionaries: Sigmund Freud and Mahatma Gandhi

All went through profound crises and then made tremendous creative gains, often accomplishing their best work. These people all grew significantly in the midst of intensive change periods in their lives. Their "lost" periods of time were often their most productive. It was as if they stumbled into greatness!

ADULT GROWTH STAGES

In achieving growth, we experience rather predictable sequences. Change follows this sequence of stages:

Stage I—Life-Cycle Plateau (e.g., the Postponed Life)

Life seems to be running pretty smoothly for us. Everything is in good working order. We may be generally satisfied with our lifestyles, relationships, careers. We could identify with Jack (p. 12–13) that things aren't going badly; they are just going. In this stage we might tend to narrow the scope and variety of our lives. Of all the exciting options we might pursue, we settle on a fixed few. We become set in our ways. Self-oblivion sets in. We lose the capacity to see what is before us, lose our freshness of perception. We postpone!

Stage II—Triggering Events

Suddenly things change—voluntarily or involuntarily. We are knocked off balance by a turn of events that reveals new problems. Turn to page 68 in chapter 9 and review the most common triggering events. Triggering events are similar to those events—those "moments of truth" or revelations—we all experience on occasion. These "awakening" events can act as catalysts to change and renewal. They may be startling, or we may just wake up one morning knowing we can't continue in the same way.

Stage III—Limbo

To insulate ourselves against the shock of abrupt change, we often go into a sort of suspended animation or limbo. We withdraw emotionally. Limbo is a feeling of knowing what your life *isn't* going to be in the future, but not having any notion of what it *is* going to be, i.e., feeling immersed in the "slish!" Being in limbo is being immobilized—trapped, without options, not knowing in which direction to turn. In time, limbo becomes boring and frustrating. We must do something—act, do anything to escape from our dilemma!

Stage IV—The Solution

We explore solutions—counseling, a personal-growth workshop, a new relationship, a book, a job change, travel, friends, ideas, a geographical move, etc. We know the answer is out there somewhere; we just have to find it. It's just around the corner, in the next course, in a new relationship or job—or under the next rock! Our orientation is external. We explore new ways of behaving; we try on new lifestyles. We are excited one day, depressed the next. We are confused, uncertain, exuberant. We seek *the* solution that will solve our dilemma and make us ultimately happy. We eventually come to the conclusion that there is no perfect solution. Like Band-Aids, the perfect solutions we counted on never quite solve the long-term problem. Band-Aids eventually fall off! Then we must seek the next solution, and the next. The excursion process in this book will give you many skills to help you move from expecting a magic solution to the next stage of decision.

Stage V—A Decision

Eventually, the quest for ultimate solutions loses its allure, and we seek resolution. Constant exploration and growth sap our energy. We seek relief. It's time to stabilize for awhile and turn our attention to the other elements of our life that we have momentarily neglected. A decision is reached. Although perhaps not a perfect decision, we start from there. Our decision might take one of three forms; the first two are based on fear and will not result in a healthy change unless more action is taken:

1. *Fight:* We decide to stay put and make the best of the "slish" we're in. Hanging on, however, we chronically complain about our situation and wish again for *the* solution to appear. We race back to the security of the "old familiar spot." Back to our postponement games. Back to the life-cycle patterns of Stage I. We quit too soon, and eventually we're hounded by another triggering event yet more frightening than the last one.

2. *Flight:* We make a lifestyle or career change according to "the book" and go through all the outward motions. Inside nothing has changed, no new self-assessment has occurred, renewal has not been real, and we are once again stuck. There is a lot of outward activity, but no inner renewal.

3. *Renewal:* We recognize that *the* solution does not exist, that life is a series of changes, each one moving us further upward in the excursion spiral. As a result, we are more accepting of our experiences. We move ahead with our decisions, more confident of our own worth and confident about the future.

Stage VI—The Inventurous Life

When we decide to renew ourselves, we often get an awakening or a "blinding glimpse of the obvious." We see more clearly the purpose and meaning of our lives. "Aha! I have finally discovered the secret to life: there is no secret! Why didn't somebody explain that to me earlier?" As one thirty-three-year-old inventurer put it:

- "The discovery is . . . I am on an excursion! Life is an upward spiral, a series of changes—the life spiral will end some day and I will die. If I keep growing, I live more fully. Life is a mystery to be lived, not an objective to be accomplished."

The inventurous life calls for plans, a map, and self-assessment. After all, you would not expect a person to design a complex building without a blueprint or after just a week-long training program in architecture. Yet often we expect ourselves to be a different person—an inventurer, perhaps—from just reading a book like this. It is one thing to understand the inventurous life; it is quite another to map your own.

You are about to set out on one of the truly fun excursions of a lifetime—that of an inventurer. The symbol of the inventurer's life and the excursion process is the expanding spiral (fig. 3.1). You have probably already seen it on your map and in various sections of the book. The spiral is many thousands of years old. The symbol originated in China to represent energy rising toward spiritual enlightenment. We have chosen to use the symbol to represent the blending of Eastern and Western thought and to reintroduce the ancient meanings of natural renewal and energy rising in a constant pattern of growth.

THE INVENTUROUS LIFE:

The hypothesis of the inventurous life is that you continue growing, expanding, and getting better as you age—that you gain optimum balance and fuller functioning as a human being as you face crises, make choices, and find goals and objectives that have value and meaning for you. Meaning in life helps you to integrate imperfect solutions to career options.

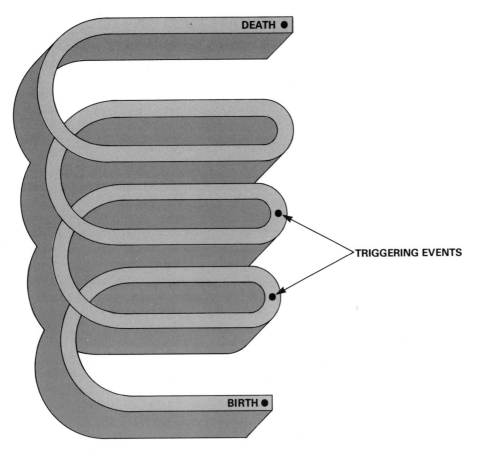

Figure 3.1.   The inventurous life cycle.

PUT YOUR MONEY WHERE YOUR MOUTH IS

From time to time throughout this book, you will be asked to stop what you are doing—whether it be reading, thinking, writing, imagining, dreaming, or conjuring—and actually get a taste of "inventure" by taking a risk and pushing yourself to draw a few conclusions, make a few decisions, and *act on them.*

Some of you will complain that the excursion process doesn't fit you or your situation or that you can't change, because other people won't let you ("they" again). If you're going to excuse yourself, at least take personal responsibility for it and don't blame others.

Contracting with another person to accomplish something by a certain date is a creative way to stimulate action on your part and overcome the villain—procrastination. At important points throughout the book, there will be contracts for you to complete. The more specific the contract, the better it is and the easier it is to know when it's been completed. It doesn't have to be elaborate, but it must describe what you will do, how you'll do it, and possible obstacles, rewards, and dates.

Commitment to clearly stated goals leads to achievement of those goals. Yet achieving commitment is not as easy as it sounds. Obstacles get in your way. Other activities compete for your time. That's why contracts are such helpful tools.

There are some guidelines for making contracts work for you. The most effective contracts are:

1. *Written:* The primary purpose of writing contracts is not so they can be shown to others, but rather to clarify them for you. Once a contract is written, you have more investment in it.

2. *Step by step:* Break your goal down into "bite-sized" pieces.

3. *Time conscious:* Setting target dates for the completion of each step of a contract provides constant reinforcement and a sense of accomplishment.

4. *Supportive:* Sharing your contract with another person helps you to clarify your thinking, obtain feedback, and generate a commitment to complete the task.

5. *Your own:* Your goals must be your own and be based on your personal values.

Here's your chance to take the first step! Decide whom you would like to contract with—(spouse, friend, coworker, manager, etc.). Say that you are asking for a commitment on that person's part to help you complete this book. Say what you need to do—the hours it will take and how much you need the other to help you stick to this task. Then mark down on your calendar regular times when you will meet together. Ask your contract partner to check on your progress and to question you if you've done little or nothing since your previous meeting.

Excursion Contract

Goal: What do I want to accomplish? Result expected?

Learn to play the harmonica. Ability to play harmonica

Action steps: What will I do to accomplish these results?   *Target dates:* By when?

1. _Buy harmonica._   _Dec. 15_
2. _Play it whenever possible._   _ongoing_
3. _start taking lessons_   _Feb 14, '89_
4. _____   _____
5. _____   _____

Obstacles: What are my favorite obstacles that I let get in the way (time, money, other people, self-image, experience, etc.)?

Not buying one.
Shyness of playing in front of people.
Time for lessons.

Reward: What do I get when I finish?

1) Connection to my soul   _4) feeling of renewal, newness_
2) Appreciation for art and creativity.
3) Means of artistic expression.

Penalty: What if I don't finish?

1) Feeling of failure to renew
2) Embarassment from others I've said "I'll do it" to.

_____
Completion date

Today's date contract
written: 12/4/88

Daniel Kwirt
My signature

_____
My partner's signature

Life Excursions

II

Adult Life Stages

4

By now you have a keen awareness of life as change and change as growth. You probably wonder if there will be *any* calm periods at all in your life. Of course there will be. The point is not to spend your whole life in pursuit of a false sense of calm.

Recent research work on the adult life cycle has given us a much better perspective for viewing life's changes—those we create and those imposed on us from the outside. The research findings so far are tentative. They are an attempt to explain the normal life patterns.

We know a great deal about how children grow and develop from birth through adolescence. Popular books remind us of the "terrible twos," "fearless fours," "noisy nines," etc. But there still are few books that explain adequately the natural development of the adult. Adults presumably just emerge from their cocoons like butterflies at age twenty or so, ready to live rational, logical, steady existences. The notion was that whereas children grow in leaps and bounds, adults only age (until the seven-year itch, as folklore has it). Research conducted mostly on men's lives and reported by Levinson, Gould, Valliant, Sheehy, and others, shows that men experience predictable life stages, although they all have unique patterns, depending on their personalities, life situations, cultural backgrounds, and life events.

There are also cycles within stages. Adulthood is a period of active and systematic change over one's lifetime. There seem to be special developmental tasks in each phase of life triggering "teachable moments" of peak readiness to move life forward.

Women's lives, however, are more difficult to predict. Iris Sangiuliano, in *In Her Time,* describes in vivid simplicity the dilemmas of the American women she spoke with.

*Woman, any woman, almost always leads a serial
life. . . . Her life is never a straight line. Women's lives
are bound by common threads. By and large, we postpone
ourselves. We live a life derived from the male experience,
whether we perceive the world through the kitchen
window or the rungs of the corporate ladder. Woman
invents herself around a man . . . intimacy precedes and
postpones a separate identity.*

Then how do women grow and develop?

*Most of us need to be transplanted . . . before we
blossom. Simply, we grow and develop through
contradiction and conflict and paradox. We grow, not
through common, predictable transitions . . . but
through the unpredictable events, those central critical
events that dislodge and shock. How we perceive these
shocks and what we do with them determines our
development.*

This may not be true for all women, of course, but it certainly holds true for
many. Full-time career women may find themselves identifying with both
male and female life-stage ideas, and feel confused as a result. Our own
informal research shows that a continuing critical issue for women is balance
between life and work, family and career, and that this is more intense and
disquieting in the midthirties.

The questions we will be asking you to reflect on as you read through
this information are, "What life stage or life event do I most identify with at
this time?" And how is this affecting the rest of my life?"

The following is a brief outline of the stages of adult development with
associated tasks for each stage. As you read them, remember that the ages
we assigned to each stage are flexible, e.g., some people experience the midlife
reassessment earlier than thirty-nine, others later than forty-six, but most of
us experience it some time. You may even experience the stages in a different
order from that which we've described.

STAGES OF ADULTHOOD*

Provisional Adulthood (Ages 22–28)

During this stage, you are building the first life system of your own and are
making your first commitments to work, marriage and family, and other adult
responsibilities. During provisional adulthood, you first put to use all of the

---

*These stages are a compilation of the work of Roger Gould, Daniel Levinson, Erik Erikson,
and Gail Sheehy. Women's lives are described more clearly in the work of Iris Sangiuliano,
Maggie Scarf, Ann Wilson Schaef, and Ellen Goodman. See the bibliography.

parental upbringing, education, and advice that was part of the childhood and adolescent growth process. In the quest to answer the question "What do you do?" we try out the "shoulds" and "oughts" of our upbringing to reach for our own identity. Rarely analyzing commitments, it's a time to explore the real world of career, marriage, lifestyle, etc.

Age Thirty Transition (Ages 29–32)

During this transition stage, initial commitments to a life system are often reexamined and their meaning questioned. The surface bravado of the provisional period wavers as life begins to look more complex. Many times you will become impatient with the early choices made and will feel a new vitality springing from within to answer the question "What do I really want out of life?" Careers and marriages become particularly vulnerable to reassessment. Long-range implications of continuing with current career, community, and life system are challenged. In many people change will occur, and in many others there will be a renewed commitment and reaffirmation of their current career, life system, and community.

Rooting (Ages 32–39)

After going through the age-thirty transition, you will tend to buckle in tentatively to the life system that has been chosen, with a more definite attitude toward it. It is a time when you might seek a mentor—a patron or supporter to "show you the ropes."

Since so much of our identity is defined in terms of our work, we tend to spend a lot of our time working. In fact, there is often not enough time, it seems, for anything but work. Focused on money and career success, we try to make our mark through career achievement and hard work. In the midst of our striving we worry about becoming trapped, about others finding out I'm not as good as they thought I was, about messing up my personal and family life. Women feel stronger contradictory pulls than men during this time because this is a prime family time.

At some point, the time squeeze begins. Perhaps it is the first emotional awareness that death will come and that time is running out. You now want more than ever to be established.

When you start out on your career or family you establish certain goals and dreams. Some of these are attainable and desirable and others are not. This time squeeze during the rooting process begins to worry you. "Is there still time to change?" Uncertain about objectives and ambivalent about values, we need time to reassess.

Midlife Transition (Ages 39–46)

This is a period which for many has been labeled as midcareer or midlife crisis. It is often a period of acute personal discomfort in which you may face the gap between youthful dreams and actual fulfillments. Likely limits of success and achievement in life and work become more apparent. There may be a difference between what you have reached and what you want. For some people, transition is merely a decade milestone. For others, however, it's a painful time of crisis. It's a lonely time, because each person is ultimately alone on the journey. You face the fact that you will die and that there are no guarantees. You look back on your life realizing you had no control over it really, and as you look ahead death frightens you.

Children are growing up and going away, and for many their parents are now looking to them for support. They are "getting it from both ends." You will often ask many self-searching questions in this period, such as "What's in it for me?" "When am I having fun?" "Why can't I be accepted for what I am, not what 'they' (spouse, boss, society) expect me to be?" "Is there one last chance to make it big?" In the search for answers, that often consumes the midlife transition period, you may turn to a new career or other new directions in life. You may live out life dramas that you haven't finished.

There is no way to sail through this reassessment. It is deeper and harder than you have experienced before. And it is hard to describe to someone who has yet to experience it. Sometimes the only thing you know for sure is that you know nothing for sure.

Restabilization and Renewal (Ages 46–54)

Once you've gone through the midlife transition satisfactorily, faced mortality, and forged a new life system, this stage might feel like the best time of life. Often unrushed by the sense of urgency of the thirties, a new stability is achieved. Adjusting to the realities of work, one may feel finally, "I have it all together." I feel secure enough to stop running and struggling. Work, perhaps, is no longer the single source of my identity. I'm not so concerned with what others think of me. It's easier to relax, open myself to new feelings, enjoy vacations. Launching children, adjusting to an empty nest, and handling increased demands of older parents are often tasks of this stage.

A career often takes on new meaning. Money becomes less important. Life is more stable because you listen more to the inner voice than to external demands. You may experience increasing attention to a few old values and a few friends. One hypothesis is that in this and the next stage, if you lose a spouse or close friend, you may go back into provisional-adulthood patterns, trying out life options all over again. Many women are finding their new selves in this period and have renewed energy, which can be mystifying to their partners. It seems like a revolving door, with men coming in and women going out.

Integration (Ages 55–64)

At this stage, people become more satisfied with themselves, coming to grips with what they have and haven't done. Delighted to see the vigor of life continuing, you often reengage with more energy into relationships, family, or community. Your concern is more with the "quality of life." You often feel a new tolerance for and companionship with your mate. A renewed focus on the spiritual dimension is also common. Eventually questions arise as to when to retire, what to do, and how to cope with sudden changes in lifestyle. It is a difficult step because nearly all of men's lives is attuned to work. Thus an abrupt shift to leisure is often traumatic. The impact of this decision is compounded by aging, termination of long-time associations and friendships, and frequently a total lack of preparation.

New Beginnings (Age 65 +)

Retirement is a stage that has been postponed—put out of mind—both by society and individuals. It cannot be postponed much longer. There are more Americans older than sixty-five at this moment than the sum of all Americans to have reached·that age in the 205 years since the country was founded! No life stage has a sharper line than the arbitrary one between those who are "active" and those who are "retired." Is retirement the best thing to ever happen? Or could it be the worst—the secret fear of many? An important step will be taken when preretirement planning includes more of the *reality* of retirement and less of the *mythology* of retirement.

For many people, the last third of life is a balance of play, continuing education, and work. But this work is often self-assigned, the work to which one had perhaps been drawn to all one's life, the work one would do for nothing—the work of freedom. A goal and a purpose and a sense of achievement equal to, and perhaps surpassing, the goal and purpose of "career work" is a search for many. We need the models—the everyday heroes and heroines—of retirement to urge us on.

Some of the tasks after sixty-five include managing leisure time, seeking new achievement outlets, searching for meaning (claiming a legacy for one's life), reconciling one's spiritual nature and being reconciled to death. We are just beginning to realize that if we don't understand retirement, we probably don't understand the rest of human existence either.

Using the excursion symbol as a representation of the life cycle, review your own position on the spiral (fig. 4.1).

Enter your life stages on the excursion map (Box 2).

WHO SHOULD I BE?

In our early life stages we spend so much of life asking that question over and over again. People asked, "What do you want to be?" We answered with one of our fantasies (e.g., professional football player, nurse, firefighter) or with answers that fit our families expectations.

Directions: Place an "X" on the spot in the model that best represents your present life position by age; place an "O" on the spot that represents the stage you identify with emotionally.

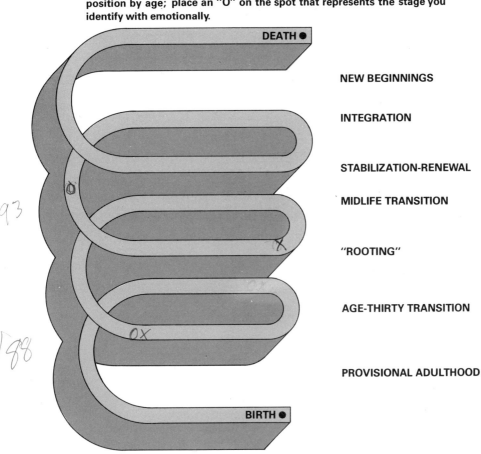

Figure 4.1. Excursion model.

In early adulthood, the search continued, but the questions hit hard and fast. Who do we want to marry? Do we want children? How many? Where do we want to live? To work? Often, answers came before we were ready.

As things settled into a pattern and we entered the thirties and forties decades, the old question arose again. What do we want to be? For some the revival of that old question creates upheaval in their lives. They had been following society's dictated route without thinking where it might end.

Inventurers learned that the question is not "*What* do we want?" It is "*Who* are we and what do we need to help us be more completely who we are?"

Knowing the question, we come closer to the answer. While the journey of self-discovery never ends, during the second half of our lives we know more certainly what questions to ask.

Use the following questions to help you think more specifically about your life stage and its issues for you. Write in your responses.

12/11/88

1. How are you *most* different today from four years ago?
   Not married. Free to choose from a multitude of paths. Happy and accomplished in my work.

2. The thing that has surprised me most about this stage of my life is:
   The ease of divorce. The excitement too.
   My ability to accept, change and (if not change) compensate for my imperfections/problems.

3. Three turning points in my life have been:
   Sweden trip.
   Getting fired.
   Divorce.

4. An issue at this phase of my life that I avoid looking at is:
   Deciding what I really want.

5. The five people who have had the deepest effect on my life to date are:
   Darby Nelson   Mom
   Marcheta   Bob
   Dad

6. As I look down the road, a "successful" life for me is one that:
   Includes: (1) a loving, stable family.
   (2) A good satisfying job
   (3) Open, fun, adventuresome

7. The most important thing, to me, at this phase, about my work is:
   Managing people.

Learning Styles

5

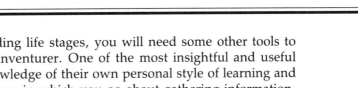

In addition to understanding life stages, you will need some other tools to aid you in becoming an inventurer. One of the most insightful and useful tools for adults is the knowledge of their own personal style of learning and changing. The personal way in which you go about gathering information, sorting it out, and making decisions is called your *learning style*. You are more likely to succeed on your excursions if you are aware of your most enjoyable learning style.

Now, no one likes being categorized, but most of us enjoy getting personal information about our uniqueness. Often we see other people making exciting changes and we get a little jealous. We think that if we'd just do what they did, it would satisfy us; but then we try doing it their way, only to find that it doesn't work for us.

DROPPING BACK IN

Jean and Don were urban dwellers who were sick of the pollution and the long work days of corporate life. With two small children and lots of exciting ideas about the good life, they followed several of their friends to the farm life in a small community 200 miles north of the largest city in their state. They planted their garden and dug in. The first year there was a drought, the refrigerator stopped, and a whole section of fencing needed replacement. They realized how unprepared they were for farm life. They didn't know what skills and techniques would be necessary or the emotional state of mind one must have to cope with nature. They returned to a "near" urban setting with a large yard and a big garden. Don took a job with a smaller firm.

Jean and Don learned a great deal from their experience, but they could have saved a lot of time and emotional and financial tumult by understanding better their own style of change and learning. After reflecting together, they now test out ideas by talking to people who have done what they want to do, read and think about questions they'll have, and then experiment on a pilot basis. We are all unique in our styles, and we approach life excursions differently. Some of us run after life, others touch life as it goes by, others observe and digest life, others meet it head on. Whatever your personal learning style, it is important to know it so you can maximize your life and career renewal.

First, let's put your learning style in an interesting and fun perspective. Many of us are intimidated by learning because we know so little about it. Think of the simple Dr. Seuss-like metaphor of each of us as a "learning gizmo" (fig. 5.1). A learning gizmo is a creative machine that takes in all kinds of information, adds some necessary ingredients, mixes everything together, and sends out a response.

As you go about the renewal process, you will be constantly taking in information, learning, and changing—like a learning gizmo. You gather information about people, places, events, and ideas by using your senses of smell, taste, touch, sight, and hearing as well as other senses which we know little about.

All of that information goes into the gizmo to be sorted out. In order to process or digest the information, you use four major abilities. *We all have these four abilities,* but each of us uses them in different ways and to different degrees. The four abilities are the basis for your *learning style.*

1. *Feeling:* Some of us choose and digest learning information primarily because it feels good (we "just know" it when we feel it). We use our emotions or feelings to guide us in deciding what to do in situations and how to proceed. We may use more body movement and speech to learn and communicate. We like having real experiences to get involved in.

2. *Observing:* Others of us use our imagination to observe and digest new material or ideas, seeing them in new ways or drawing mind pictures. We would rather think through ideas using visuals and analogies or write about ideas than verbalize off the tops of our heads. We react to the ideas of others.

3. *Thinking:* Still others of us primarily scrutinize or analyze information, pulling it apart and putting it back together logically. We design models and symbols, taking as much information into account as possible.

Figure 5.1. Learning gizmo.

4. *Acting:* Some of us see information primarily as part of action, to help solve a problem. We use words and acts to promote a project or a solution. We like to learn while it's happening. We make things happen.

One of the problems with most life and career or other personal-growth programs is that they are taught on the basis of only one major style. Some inventurers like charts and graphs. But for others, charts are like sudden death. Some like pushing themselves in a group; others need lots of time alone with the material. *The Inventurers* is written to take all styles into account and to encourage you to identify and then adopt exercises that suit your own style. Some exercises are written with options for each learning style.

People with different learning styles will go about the process of change and growth, or inventuring, in different ways. At points along your life excursion, you will use all of the styles in some way, but as you will find out, you are probably more interested in or more inclined toward one style.

In a minute, you will take a simple, subjective learning-style profile that we adapted and designed based on the fine work of David Kolb at Case Western University. It will help you understand your learning style better. A few introductory words to acquaint you with our intent are in order.

1. Learning profiles and personality tests are not the be-all and the end-all. They are only guides that help you capitalize on information that you probably already know at least subconsciously about yourself. There is no learning style that is better than any other; they are just different.

2. No one likes to be categorized and forever stuck in a box. Find out your favorite style, then read about the others and use them along the way too, if you choose. Your style may vary slightly in different learning situations, but not drastically.

3. Subjective (self-report) tests depend partially on your mood or state of mind when you take the test and may vary slightly if taken at another time. Don't carve your style in gold, but use it as an indicator. Other people may see you differently, depending on how well they know you. They only know what you choose to show or tell them. But ask others' opinions of you according to the learning-style descriptions and see how closely they agree with your own.

4. Your learning style may vary slightly from situation to situation, or for specific learning tasks, or you may have gained more learning experience with age. You still use basically a most preferred style, but you can shift around.

Learning-Style Inventory

As you complete this inventory, think of the ways you most frequently go about learning. If you are trying something new, how do you learn best? If you are preparing to teach other people about a topic, how do you most easily prepare yourself? Mark "A" if you strongly identify with the word on the left, "B" if less so, "C" if you identify more with the word on the right, "D" if you strongly identify with the right side. You might generally use the sentences that precede each section.

Generally, I learn best by:

	A	B	C	D	
Talking			X		Listening
Acting		X			Reacting
Taking small steps			X		Observing overall picture
Being quick			X		Being deliberate
Experimenting		X			Digesting
Carrying out ideas			X		Thinking up ideas
Changing	X				Remaining constant
Being animated				X	Being reserved
Doing	X				Watching
Being goal-oriented			X		Being process-oriented
Being practical		X			Seeing ideals
Changing as I go			X		Mapping out in advance
Finding solutions		X			Identifying problems
Formulating answers			X		Formulating questions

Total the number of As, Bs, Cs, and Ds you checked and write them below.

As _2_   Bs _4_   Cs _7_   Ds _1_

In learning situations, I am:

	1	2	3	4	
Intuitive			X		Logical
Personally involved		X			Impersonally objective
Emotional			X		Intellectual
Supportive		X			Critical
Eager to discuss with others	X				Prone to analyze by myself
Interested in new experiences		X			Interested in new ideas, models
A believer in opinion		X			A believer in theory
Accepting		X			Questioning
Feeling			X		Thinking
A quick risk taker		X			A slow risk taker
Prone to trial and error		X			Prone to planning and organizing
People-oriented		X			Task-oriented
Ready to jump in				X	Wanting facts first
Dependent			X		Independent

Total the number of 1s, 2s, 3s, and 4s (if you checked four 2s, you have a total of 4, not 8!). Write them below.

1s _1_   2s _8_   3s _4_   4s _1_

You've been asked to react to several dimensions of learning. As we sort them out, we find that people identify with some more than with others and that there are four major learning styles. Let's put the dimensions together and explain what each of the learning styles means. (See fig. 5.2.)

In learning new information, some people rely more on their feelings; others on their thoughts. Some people are very active; others are more laid back. Your scores will tell you which of these factors you favor most.

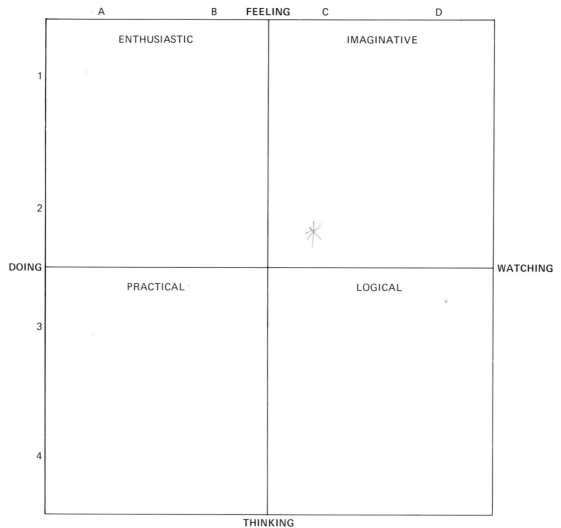

Figure 5.2.   The learning-style profile.

- *Imaginative learners:* People who are feeling-type learners, but who also are deliberate and studied.
- *Logical learners:* People who are deliberate, unhurried, and also thinkers, relating most to ideas.
- *Practical learners:* People who are thinkers and also active problem solvers.
- *Enthusiastic learners:* People who are active, involved, and also feeling-oriented.

First, look back at your learning-style inventory and find out what your total scores are. Add up the total number of As, Bs, Cs, and Ds, and 1s, 2s, 3s, and 4s. Write them below. Circle your highest score on each line. For example:

A___3___   B___⑧___   C___3___   D___0___
1___2___   2___⑦___   3___4___   4___1___
A___2___   B___4___   C___⑦___   D___1___
1___1___   2___⑧___   3___4___   4___1___

Now you need to transfer these scores to the profile in fig. 5.2. You do that in three steps.

Step 1: Draw a dotted line down the boxes, starting from your highest letter score (A, B, C, D).

Step 2: Draw a dotted line across the boxes, starting from your highest number score (1, 2, 3, 4).

Step 3: Mark with a star (*) the place where they intersect. (See example in fig. 5.3.) That is your most enjoyed learning style. The explanation for each style is in fig. 5.4.

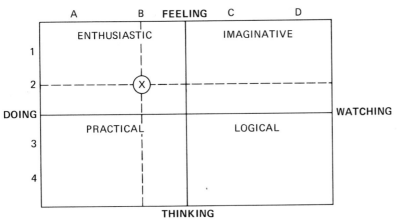

Figure 5.3.   A sample learning-style profile.

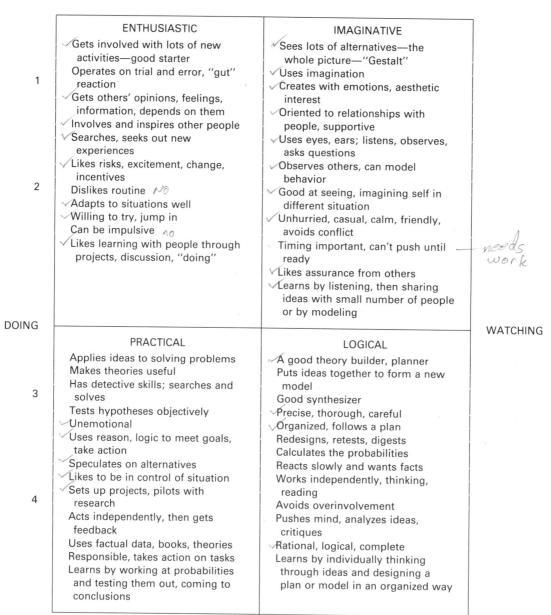

A   B   FEELING   C   D

ENTHUSIASTIC

✓ Gets involved with lots of new
   activities—good starter
Operates on trial and error, "gut"
   reaction
✓ Gets others' opinions, feelings,
   information, depends on them
✓ Involves and inspires other people
✓ Searches, seeks out new
   experiences
✓ Likes risks, excitement, change,
   incentives
Dislikes routine *NO*
✓ Adapts to situations well
✓ Willing to try, jump in
Can be impulsive *no*
✓ Likes learning with people through
   projects, discussion, "doing"

IMAGINATIVE

✓ Sees lots of alternatives—the
   whole picture—"Gestalt"
✓ Uses imagination
✓ Creates with emotions, aesthetic
   interest
✓ Oriented to relationships with
   people, supportive
✓ Uses eyes, ears; listens, observes,
   asks questions
✓ Observes others, can model
   behavior
✓ Good at seeing, imagining self in
   different situation
✓ Unhurried, casual, calm, friendly,
   avoids conflict
   Timing important, can't push until   — *needs*
   ready   *work*
✓ Likes assurance from others
✓ Learns by listening, then sharing
   ideas with small number of people
   or by modeling

PRACTICAL

Applies ideas to solving problems
Makes theories useful
Has detective skills; searches and
   solves
Tests hypotheses objectively
✓ Unemotional
✓ Uses reason, logic to meet goals,
   take action
✓ Speculates on alternatives
✓ Likes to be in control of situation
✓ Sets up projects, pilots with
   research
Acts independently, then gets
   feedback
Uses factual data, books, theories
Responsible, takes action on tasks
Learns by working at probabilities
   and testing them out, coming to
   conclusions

LOGICAL

✓ A good theory builder, planner
Puts ideas together to form a new
   model
Good synthesizer
✓ Precise, thorough, careful
✓ Organized, follows a plan
Redesigns, retests, digests
Calculates the probabilities
Reacts slowly and wants facts
Works independently, thinking,
   reading
Avoids overinvolvement
Pushes mind, analyzes ideas,
   critiques
✓ Rational, logical, complete
Learns by individually thinking
   through ideas and designing a
   plan or model in an organized way

DOING   WATCHING

THINKING

Figure 5.4.   Learning-styles explanation.

If you have ties, it means that you just see yourself between two styles. If the tie is between "B" and "D," you are probably "C." If you score in the corner of any quadrant (A_1, D_1, D_4, A_4), it means that you identify very strongly with that style.

Ask other people to do the inventory on you too, so that you can compare their scores with yours. If you are going through a major change in your life, you may overreact to yourself and alter your style, but usually you are pretty consistent.

Remember, only you can decide whether or not you will make changes. This book gives you the tools to use *when* you decide to do it! One of the most important tools is your learning style, and that's why we chose to introduce you to your own style early in the book. Flexibility, or the ability to use many styles of learning, depending on the situation, is a goal to strive for. The more you can shift when you need to, the more satisfied you might be with your overall learning. But remember, you still have a preferred style that you will identify with primarily. *Now you know your preferred style, and you can use it throughout the excursion process.*

To assist you, we've developed symbols representing each learning style. In addition to the information you already know about how you learn and change, you can refer to these symbols periodically at the end of exercises or chapters to modify the experience and use your best style to increase or maximize your prospects for learning and change.

They would enjoy "doing" this process with others, talking about the exercises, and trying out several options at once. The process will excite them to test gut reactions and schemes.

Enthusiastic

Imaginatives like to do the exercises and then let them soak in for a while before acting on them. They will watch what others do and imagine themselves doing the same to see how it feels.

Imaginative

A thorough, planned approach to the process is most comfortable for logicals. After doing all the exercises and some from other books too, they will wonder how to take action on it all.

Logical

Practicals will scan the book for the exercises that seem most relevant for now. They will finish what they wanted and develop likely options with a plan of attack, before asking how this will affect others.

Practical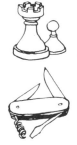

Learning-Style Examples

We need to learn how to laugh at ourselves more frequently and more easily. Each learning style has its positive traits and its problems. The following chart shows the typical reactions that different learning styles exhibit in different situations.

Enter your learning style on the excursion map (Box 3).

	Approaching a new job	Turning in reports	Learning to ride a ten-speed bike	Learning a language
Enthusiastic	Meets the people. Gets the office looking friendly. Finds the lunchroom.	Prefers verbal reporting. Hates writing long detailed reports. Accepts short notice if notes and outlines are sufficient.	Jumps on and doesn't read directions. Expects to be rescued. An opportunity to meet a new person.	Lives in with a family. Goes to a country and explores it.
Imaginative	Tours the office. Knows who's who. Gets a "feel" for the environment. Asks questions, observes.	Prefers charts, maps, and pictures. Likes to have longer notice. Uses analogies.	Goes to park to observe people riding. Asks a neighbor how he or she does it. "Images" self on bike.	Uses language tapes. Reads lips.
Logical	Reads the manual. Finds out the rules. Looks at the organizational chart. Reads the annual report. Organizes desk and files.	Prefers lead time and clear expectations. Will write tomes, so needs limits Likes graphs, graphs, graphs, and charts. Is well organized.	Reads instructions on riding and does it. Takes only ten minutes and eliminates most error.	Takes a university course on grammar and reading.

	Approaching a new job	Turning in reports	Learning to ride a ten-speed bike	Learning a language
Practical	Finds out who does what, and where the power is. Finds problems to start solving. Gets a good assistant to file and organize.	Prefers knowing why the report is needed and when. Answers key questions with evidence, cases. Keeps reports short and to the point. Will talk you through it.	Takes instruction book but only looks up the necessary part. Keeps it in back pocket for future reference.	Takes a short course on conversational language. Uses sleep records.

Alone
Together

6

Rarely will you find anyone who has been through a major life or career reconsideration totally alone. There is always someone to read about, talk to, share feelings with, ask advice of, react to. But for each individual, the kinds and numbers of these people are different. When it comes right down to making decisions, making changes, starting to grow, *you* are still the only one who has control (even though you choose to abdicate it to others sometimes). It is the people around you, however, who can be the best catalysts, prodders, listeners, provokers, and models. Many people find that people around them are also obstacles, weights, discouragers, and martyrs. For serious inventurers, it is important to scrutinize your personal relationships—not scrap them, but cultivate people who will be supportive during the change. For many people, this means some new friends.

One of your best supporters, of course, could be you! Unfortunately, many of us rarely take the time to even get to know ourselves in simple ways such as journal writing, trips alone, or even walks alone. In Outward Bound Life and Career Renewal groups, individuals spend thirty-six hours on a solo, alone in the wilderness, listening, thinking, writing. Some people say that it takes up to fifteen hours just to get the ringing of the city noise out of their ears. Then they can begin to hear the wilderness sounds much better. If you have never been on a "solo" experience, plan now to take some time (two hours, an afternoon, a day, a weekend) to be by yourself. You could start by eating out or going to a park, another town, the woods, or across the country. This can be a very exhilarating experience. At first, a lot of fears and other buried feelings may emerge. Start with small increments of time and more structured activities. It can be even more significant if you record your reactions.

INVENTURE NETWORK

There are three major categories of people who will be useful to you on your inventure. You will need all of them sometime during the trip, and some of them will be major forces in your life. The three groups together are called an *inventure network* (fig. 6.1). Let's take each of these categories of people separately, define them, and look at how other people have used each of them in their excursions.

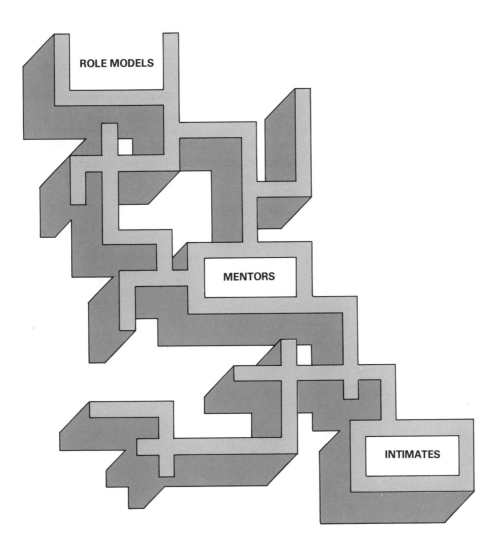

ROLE MODELS

MENTORS

INTIMATES

Figure 6.1.   The inventure network.

Role Models

These people fit the image of what you'd like to be. They may not even know you, but you identify with some characteristics that you like in them. They represent a standard you are aiming for that will help you set goals and mark progress. We generally use models for change in two steps. First, we recognize what qualities in that person we like or want; second, we imagine or imitate the behavior in our minds.

Many people will not make changes in their lives until they can "see" themselves in the new image. They must imagine themselves speaking in front of a group, finishing school, winning a race, not smoking, hitting a golf ball. Until they can accept themselves in the new image, they won't change. Role models, or respected images, are important in forming the new behavior that you want to cultivate, and for many they are the first step toward change.

Frank had a difficult time speaking smoothly before a group of people. He had all the organizational skills, but he just panicked before he was about to go on. He observed a very accomplished speaker carefully to see how he started the speech, what he did with his hands and his facial expressions, how he "read" the audience. Then, right before his next speech, Frank went to the large room where the meeting was to be held and imagined himself as the man he had observed. He imagined what the audience would be like. He went to the podium and stood behind it, looking out over the imagined audience. Finally, he rehearsed the whole scene in his head and spoke out loud occasionally, just to hear himself. He finished the speech and anticipated the response. Then he made any changes that had occurred to him during rehearsal. The next day, he had the experience of a lifetime. The speech went exceptionally well—after all, it was the second time he had given it to the same audience!

Think of people (alive or dead) whom you consider role models—people having some characteristics or qualities (personal, intellectual, athletic, spiritual, emotional) you'd like to imitate. Your role models can be friends, teachers, novelists, sports heroes, spouses, parents, historical figures. Enter the names of your role models in the appropriate network spaces in fig. 6.2, p. 47.

Mentors

Mentors have been described as "what most people are missing in their life excursions." Recently, it has been discovered that women and minorities in the business world generally lack mentors. But it has also been discovered that *most* people cannot identify their mentors. The questions then arise: What are mentors? Where do you find one?

Mentors are people you consider wise and trustworthy individuals, those who serve as your advisers, guides, or counselors in helping you fulfill your potential. The term "mentor" comes from a Greek legend about Mentor, a friend and adviser of Odysseus and a guardian of his son. Mentor's role was to motivate others and help them accomplish their goals.

Mentors first and foremost are *good listeners*. They can wear a number of hats in relation to your excursion. Mentors, like role models, can be colleagues, teachers, religious leaders, friends, relatives, spouses, social acquaintances, or supervisors. Their main role is to help you to reflect, grow, wait, change, or whatever you need to do to reach your personal or professional potential.

Mentors can be recognized by the things they do (or by the things you want them to do):

- They listen.
- They ask questions.
- They further develop your plans.
- They influence, but don't determine, your plans.
- They help you solve problems.
- They expect you to use your own best judgment.
- They help you find your own skills and potential.
- They do not expect you to be "just like they are."
- They challenge and prod you.
- They support and trust you.
- They give you advice on technical or organizational matters, serving as expert resources.
- They share your ups and downs.
- They provide you with realistic personal information.

Mentors can be cultivated—and sometimes have to be. Few people have thought seriously of having a mentor. Fewer yet have thought about acting as a mentor to someone else. So there may be a mentor in your life that you just don't recognize as such. Or you may realize that you don't have a mentor. Now is the time to look for a person who can fulfill some of the expectations listed above. It may take time and some effort, but it's well worth it. People who have successfully made lifestyle or career changes say that at crucial times, the people around them, including mentors, made an enormous difference in their outlook and on their persistence.

Jane had wanted to start her own private counseling practice for a whole year. She had been working as a counselor (psychologist) in a treatment center for six years and had gained enough experience and reputation to work on her own. She knew the overhead costs, start-up costs, the principles she'd use, and even the professional referrals she could count on for clients. But there was something missing—action. Every few months, she met with a long-term friend, an older, more experienced person in another profession, to share ideas and digest new insights. At their meeting, he asked her about work and she replied, "I need a place to work and my first client." He said, "If I can help you find a place, can you get the clients?" Needless to say, she started her private practice on a part-time basis within six weeks.

Bill was really getting bored by the kinds of skills he was using on his job within a large foods firm. After four years, he'd got the job so well refined that he could do it without much challenge. He talked with a colleague from another company who had recently made a job shift within that company. They went over his skills, abilities, and interests and decided in which direction he should go. He wanted to work as part of a team on a new product within his division. He was excited about the prospects and talked to his supervisor about it. His balloon burst. His supervisor didn't see any possibilities like that at the present time, although he really agreed with Bill's assessment and proposal. Bill *decided* not to give up and went back to his colleague to plan the next steps. He decided to talk informally to other people at work about his ideas. After many conversations over weeks, he was getting discouraged. At lunch one day, he saw an old colleague from another department, and they began to share ideas. The projects he was interested in were actually being started in another place within the company. He knew immediately that his opportunity had come. He worked for weeks with his supervisor and the other department head arranging for a transfer. It worked, and in time he was doing what he wanted to do—a much happier man.

Jean had been home, raising three small children for the first twelve years of her marriage. Her youngest was in school now, and she had a lot of time on her hands. At church one Sunday, she just happened to mention her dilemma to an older friend who explained, "That's exactly how I felt when my kids went to school, but I didn't do anything about it for years!" As they talked, it dawned on Jean that she really wanted to return to school to finish her B.A. degree. Her friend knew several resources at local adult-oriented college programs and served as a source of referral and support for the next six months. Jean put together an art and counseling program that she'd been thinking about for years as a result of her community experiences with adolescent drop-in centers. Her mentor continued to encourage her, and their friendship grew at the same time. They may eventually start a small pilot art program for youth at their church.

Now it's time for you to consider your own mentors. Remember, mentors can be community leaders, colleagues, or supervisors who are interested in your growth and will encourage and push you; they can be experts in an area who can provide you with information or direction; or they can be other people who are just willing to listen, share, support, advise, and guide. They should be people you trust and respect. Your needs for mentors will change. You may have a mentor and be a mentor at the same time. If you don't have a mentor, here are some suggestions for finding one.

1. Go to professional meetings. Consider your professional colleagues.
2. Talk to speakers at conferences.
3. Cultivate teachers.
4. Look over your holiday card list for "sleepers."
5. Think of people at work whom you respect and enjoy talking to.
6. Consider community colleagues, political friends, PTA members, musical groups, church affiliates, committee members, club members, civic group members, arts organization members.
7. Don't overlook sports partners.
8. Use impersonal sources such as novelists and columnists.
9. Consider family members—brothers, sisters, aunts, uncles, parents.
10. Always be alert in new situations. Mentors lurk in the most unsuspecting places—airports, supermarkets, barbershops.

Enter the names of your mentors in the appropriate network space in fig. 6.2, p. 47.

Intimates

Intimates are a very special part of your inventure network; they are your closest, warmest, truest, and most important friends. They stick with you "no matter how tough the going gets." It isn't always easy for them to be around when you are going through changes, especially when it seems as though you'll never get out of limbo; but remember, they're around for the celebrations too. You can share anything with these people and not be afraid or embarrassed. You can trust and depend on them—because they care about you.

Usually this group of people is quite small—spouse, partner, best friend, neighbor, or relative. Many people realize that even though they have friends or may live with someone, they have few, if any, intimates. Others think they have ten or more—only because they share their feelings freely. Most men, until recently, have thought of their intimates as their wives, lovers, or sports partners—by titles rather than by their roles as people who have shared their innermost dreams, fears, and accomplishments. Increasingly, men have allowed themselves the experience of sharing feelings, ideas, hopes, and laughter with intimates.

Intimates are not necessarily people with whom you share sexual experience, but rather people of both sexes with whom you share closeness. Intimates, too, can be cultivated—and must be attended to for the relationship to grow. Entire books could and have been written about the care and feeding of intimate relationships.

The closer the relationship is and the more important it is, the more difficult it is to establish. Most good relationships cannot be pushed—they have to evolve over time. You usually can't just walk up to someone and ask that person to be your intimate. Just being aware of the need for intimates will be the first step. People still go out to "look for dates, find their catch, fill a void." The irony of the situation is that until you look within and develop your own personal lifestyle, you won't be the kind of person who would attract the kind of person you want anyway. It's all got to start from the inside out.

If you have no intimates, mentors and friends can serve some of these needs. For the time being, you can be more aware of your interest in cultivating a deeper friendship. You may be a person who says you don't need intimates. That's possible. *If you want to make any significant changes* in your life or your work, however, intimates for support and encouragement are often *the* factor that makes the difference. Families or intimates are often profoundly affected by the changes you make, and it is crucial to let them in on your excursions at appropriate times. They will experience many of the feelings you do in the consideration of change, and if you can get their assistance and support, it may be the most enriching experience of your lives.

Here are some suggestions from other inventurers for ways to involve your intimates in the process:

- Share the book with them and have everyone do the exercises, discussing them at specific times.

- Take a long weekend away from home to discuss life plans and work options.

- Take turns making changes with other intimates, supporting each other.
- Start a book club, choosing books on change and growth.
- Form an inventurer's support group with friends, church members, and neighbors to encourage one another in your endeavors.
- Discuss these exercises with youth in their groups (teams, scouts, church groups) and get them to share their sentiments.
- Get involved in family counseling to get an objective view of your decision-making processes.
- Go slowly—all people fear change when it may have an impact on them.

There will be a category of friends, acquaintances, and relatives who will not be listed in any of the categories above—role models, mentors, intimates. They are fine friends and comrades, but will not be as crucial in your excursion. Don't forget them, but don't concentrate all your time on them! Also, some categories may overlap; some mentors may be intimates, and some role models may be mentors.

Write the names of intimates in the appropriate network space in fig. 6.2.

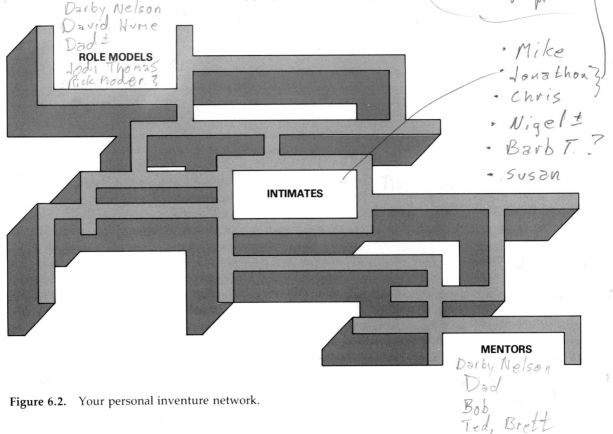

Figure 6.2.   Your personal inventure network.

Enter names of your best role models, mentors, and intimates on your excursion map (Box 4).

You can't get by with just identifying the people in your inventure network; you must make use of them to get maximum benefit. You may already be doing this, but follow along anyway.

THE DIALOGUE

Invite one of your inventure-network members who is a good listener to meet with you to start some exploration. It may be the first time you've sat down with anyone to just talk about yourself, and that's what you are about to do.

1. Actually hand over this book and have the person read the statements in the dialogue exercise that follows to you one at a time. You may want to look over the list first and think through the responses briefly before sharing them.

2. Finish the sentences out loud, and have your partner jot down the answers in the space provided.

3. Do not get into conversations about how the other person would complete the sentences. It's your turn this time.

4. When you're finished, look over your answers for any themes, recurring ideas or qualities, any new insights. Write them in the space provided; e.g., "Every time I dream about the future, I'm involved in sports" or "I'm definitely not using my best skills, the ones others recognize in me" or "I'm frustrated!"

5. Let your partner then comment.

6. If you'd like, switch roles and ask the questions of the other person.

The Dialogue Questions

1. Five words that describe my personality best are (*not* roles such as worker, wife, teacher):

2. Two feelings I never allow myself to express to others are:

3. The main, overriding concern at this stage in my life is:

4. My best childhood memory is:

5. Two perceptions of me that I don't like are:

6. The type of people I like best are:

7. The age I would be if I didn't know how old I was is:

8. Three occupations I can fantasize myself doing are:

9. If I had $1000 extra for the month, I would:

10. If I were to choose an object or concept that would describe me, it would be a (kind of car—silver Datsun, yellow VW, gold Cadillac, blue jeep; kind of weather—sunny, cloudy, stormy, hot and muggy), because:

11. Four things I dream of doing before I die are:

12. Two different places I can imagine myself wanting to live are:

13. The way I've changed most in the last five years is:

14. The person whose life I most admire is:

15. A good question for someone to ask me would be:

etc. Write any themes, insights, recurring ideas, or qualities (have your partner help you if you like).

_____

_____

_____

Enter your major dialogue insights on your excursion map (Box 5).

For Further Exploration

I'm very interested in finding out more about my image of myself. What are some ways I can pursue these activities further, using my learning style?

Interview your role model, or mentor, using some of these questions or others you choose to find out more about what makes them tick. Or compare some answers with several people around you to see how other people perceive themselves compared to you.

Think of all the different images you have of yourself (animals, plants, seasons, rooms) (question 10). Write them somewhere for safekeeping. Think about how you see others in your surroundings. Get a dialogue going in your head among the different objects. Share any insights with close friends.

Take several other personality profiles and compare your self-description on them with the interview exercise. Note any consistencies or discrepancies. (See the bibliography.)

Think of the most important thing you learned from the interview. How could you use the information you gained to make some decision you've been thinking about? Set up some kind of action or goal you can now meet as a result of your insight. Do it!

Lifestyles

III

The Balancing Act

7

"Lifestyle" is a confusing term. The word "lifestyle" often refers to some combination of the place where you live, the social life you lead, your appearance (clothes, hairstyle, and cosmetics), the people you affiliate with, the education you pursue, the places you eat, the hobbies you pursue, the books you read, and the values you reflect. Few people really agree on what it is or how to describe it. Yet in numerous career-development studies (including our own), half of the participants are making important changes in their lifestyles before they go on to career-related issues. It is clearly an important item in our lives.

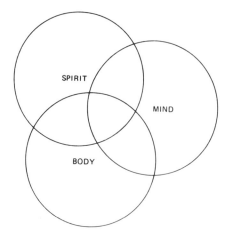

Figure 7.1. Three key ingredients of lifestyle.

Discussions of lifestyle consistently reflect three key factors—key ingredients—that must be balanced for a full and satisfying life. The three are the intellectual (mind), the physical (body), and the emotional (spirit) (fig. 7.1). If these three elements are in balance, they reinforce one another; e.g., good physical health encourages clearer thinking. If they are out of balance, they multiply problems; e.g., when you have the flu, it is hard to pick yourself up to get involved in a tough task at work.

The areas of overlap, or integration, among mind, body, and spirit are important to recognize. Each has an influence on the others, and failure to realize this can have negative effects (e.g., trying to push yourself to write a paper or project when you are emotionally exhausted). The three factors multiply their positive effects when they are in balance. Increasingly, we are learning how much control the mind and spirit can have over the body, e.g., psychosomatic illness and the effect of meditation on the body.

As a simple analogy, the three factors could be likened to the various parts of a sailboat (see fig. 7.2).

The mind: (the sailor)   There has to be a sailor or someone to control and steer the boat. The person who holds the rudder and the riggings actually determines the direction and the speed to some extent. In your life, your mind is the element that controls your functioning.

The body: (the hull)   The obvious physical structure of the boat, the hull and mast, are like your physical body. People can determine the type of boat from the structure. In your life, your physical structure and the way you care for it determine how you are seen by others.

The spirit: (the sails)   The sails which catch the wind and enable the boat to move are like your spirit—sometimes mysterious, other times cooperative,

Figure 7.2.   Three key ingredients of a sailboat.

other times flapping in the breeze. In your life, your spirit gives you the inner strength to change and grow and often has the strongest effect on your growth.

We need all three parts of the sailboat in order to move about successfully, but the movement toward some goal seems to be determined primarily by the sailor. However, the working together of all elements is necessary. The sailor depends on the sails filling and the structure being well designed.

Let's try to describe this lifestyle integration among the three factors more clearly. We can first define the factors as follows:

1. *Intellectual:* Activity and interest related to the *mind,* e.g., reading, learning, verbal communication, thinking, organizational skill, writing, intellectual creativity.

2. *Physical:* Activities and interest related to the *body,* e.g., exercise and health, strength, energy, food and nutrition, outward appearance (clothes, hair, and cosmetics), physical structures, and spaces you live in.

3. *Emotional:* Activities and interests related to the *spirit*—to feelings, attitudes, and values—e.g., personal esteem, attitudes, feelings, relationships with others, and spirituality of all kinds.

Each lifestyle factor has the potential to be positive and growth-producing. But there is a danger in overfocusing in any one area to the detriment of the others. You might get out of balance. You might lose perspective.

What happens if you live out of balance or with an area missing for long periods of time? During that time, you are an incomplete person, and eventually you might suffer from the imbalance. Here are some examples of common lifestyle imbalances:

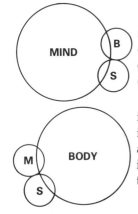

1. *Mind supreme:* These very unemotional, unspontaneous people live in such an intellectual world that there is little fun in life. They are frightened of people and situations unless they can control them rationally. They are out of shape, physically inactive, and scoff at things that are a waste of time (unintellectual), such as doing anything with their hands!

2. *Body supreme:* These people are expert at looking good and/or persistent in doing exceptionally well at physical activities. Physical appearance or physical prowess is of primary interest. These people's lives are geared toward appearances, and they are often immature intellectually and emotionally after initial contact. They are happy only during a physical chase or challenge. As they age, they get more and more frantic.

3. *Spirit supreme:* Expert at emotion, these people are often unstable and unpredictable. Their turbulent emotions rule. They feel from moment to moment and direct their lives on the basis of whims, moving from one high to the next. They seek quick solutions to increase the affect—relationships, mind-altering chemicals, creative expression, spirituality. Their self-esteem is often low because environmental happenings dictate their self-images. They tend to get swallowed personally in events, only to emerge with less and less ability to resolve things rationally. They begin to wonder about their inability to think at all.

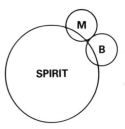

Throughout your life, there will be times when you will focus more on one area of your three life factors. Any triggering event can cause your circles to be out of balance, so can a phase of your life. Review the adult life stages mentioned in chapter 4. At a time of reassessment, age-thirty transition, for example, you may temporarily focus on the spirit factor, looking inward at values and beliefs, at spiritual ideals. Then when you are through the transition, your three factors take on more balance again, and you can throw yourself into home, work, and other activities with more intellectual and physical energy. Another example is midlife transition, when physical and emotional issues loom large. You may lean heavily in those directions for awhile (feeling at times that it'll never be over!), and one day it all looks as though it's back in perspective. Some people at this stage are so out of balance with one life factor that it is all but missing.

When one of your life factors is out of proportion, the common reaction is to put emphasis only on the swollen circle to get it back into proportion and become comfortable again. This causes more stress on that circle and can compound the original problem. It can cause you to wallow in the stress. An example would be someone who is injured in an athletic event and pushes the healing process too quickly, thus increasing the likelihood of further injury.

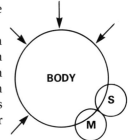

not helpful

A more effective way to cope with a swollen circle would be to put more emphasis on the other two circles, thus increasing their size and getting more balance. Using the above example, the injured person could exercise to heal appropriately, *and* focus on the ways in which these other circles could be enlarged. They might include reading, mind games, or journal writing for the mind, or music, humor, and friendships for the spirit. The body needs time to heal.

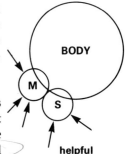

helpful

Some people develop very negative or even dangerous coping techniques that they delude themselves into accepting as effective. Their circles may not even be connected at all and they are hiding their pain. Examples of negative coping techniques might include excessive drinking, overeating, extended sleeping, reckless driving, overworking, or use of illegal drugs.

Inventurers have developed their coping techniques down to a science. They still experience stress but they know how to get themselves back into balance when they need to. You'll have a chance at the end of the lifestyle section to learn how to do that too. Inventurers choose at various times to deliberately stretch the walls of their circles, push themselves to grow, to change, to get out of balance. That's how they thrive. And if a triggering event should come along, they revert to their tried and true coping techniques to get back in balance. At some point they trust in their inner process so deeply that stress automatically is absorbed into their system, balanced, and seen as energizing from an outside perspective.

In this section, you will complete exercises in each lifestyle factor. If you are not satisfied with a factor and you want some change, you can contract to make future changes. Don't read through the section and say it won't work without working on it. That is like letting someone else decide for you that you can't change. *You* are the one who makes it work.

Are you ready to go? First, find a quiet, comfortable place away from the usual distractions. Give yourself enough time to do some writing as well as some reflection. Plan several sessions to complete the chapters in this section.

LIFESTYLE BALANCE

Start the whole process with a self-diagnosis. Draw the size of circle that represents the amount of activity of each life factor for you (body, mind, spirit). Are you completely oriented to one over the others; for instance, do you let your mind rule, always analyzing and arguing about terms, definitions, strategies, and outcomes? Or have you been at home with small children, concentrating your communication on nonverbal areas for so many years that your spirit circle is large and the others smaller? Or are you such a health fanatic that your body circle is crowding out the people in your life? Give an overall impression, not a complicated analysis (you can do that later). If you are way out of balance, do you know why? Being continually out of balance may seem comfortable for us but we are negating parts of ourselves and sooner or later we will feel the effects.

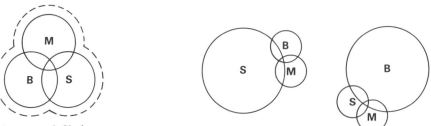

Inventurer's Choices

My Life Balance

(Draw your circles here.)

(Draw a set of circles on your excursion map (Box 6).

At the conclusion of the lifestyle section, come back to this page and draw another set of circles to see if your perception has changed.

Life-Cycle Review

8

It is sometimes difficult to live a fully satisfying life until you have had a close personal awareness of your own death. Iugore states, *"Death belongs to life as birth does. The walk is in the raising of the foot as in the laying of it down."* The whole concept of death and dying is very frightening to most of us. Yet those who have ultimately known people who are dying or have experienced their own deaths through unique physical, psychological, or psychic experiences have found their lives profoundly altered as a result. For all of us, the last stage of our life-cycle growth is death, the bottom line.

Life-Cycle Review

The Life-Cycle Review Exercise, using the excursion model in fig. 8.1, shows the relationship of your life to the general adult life stages, the ongoing excursions you experience from birth to death. Let's begin by putting your life into a larger context.

1. Next to the death point, write the age you think you will be when you die and the year in which it will occur.

2. Write the probable cause of your death.

3. Mark the approximate midpoint of your life. Write the age you will be (were) at the midpoint. Mark the approximate place you are now. Write your present age next to it. How far along are you in your life? Halfway? Three-fourths? One-fourth?

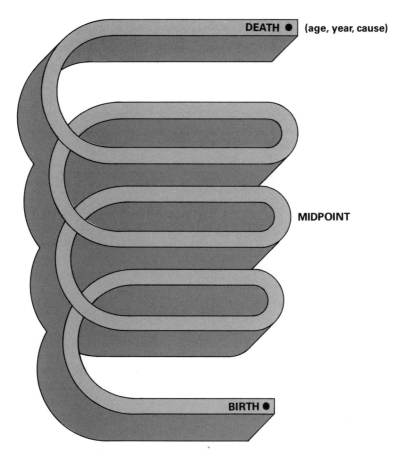

Figure 8.1.   Excursion model.

4. Some people experience a definite time in their lives when they moved from external expectations to internal considerations, a deepening and a move toward self-esteem. Draw a line cutting through the model at the place in which you decided to be in charge of your life, to take control and responsibility, to become an inventurer. If you haven't done this yet, predict when you will.

Life-Image

Now it's time to think about your life in more detail. Everyone will have a different way of going about this so we've suggested alternatives for each learning style and have given you a sample of each. Pick the format that's most intriguing and settle in for some real insights.

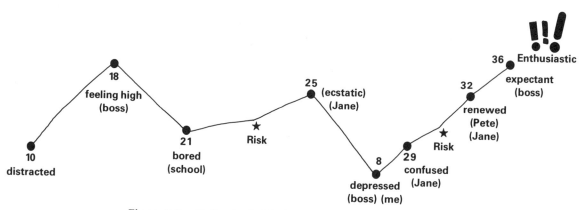

Figure 8.2. Enthusiastic life image.

Complete the exercise verbally by telling your life story to someone else and/ or tape recording it. Consider people who have influenced you, different feelings you've had during stages of your life, risks you've taken, and peak experiences. Look at your life as a line. When has the line been up (feeling good), and when has it been down (feeling bad)? (See fig. 8.2.)

Review your life in your mind before writing it. Think of your whole life as a movie or play, with different segments as acts and scenes. Visualize scenes by thinking of houses you've lived in, schools you've attended, jobs you've had, key events that affected you. Or think of your life as an object, like a train or a box (fig. 8.3).

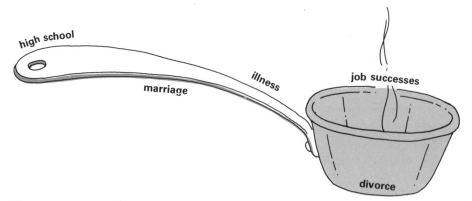

Figure 8.3. Imaginative life image.

Complete the exercise by dividing your life into two- or three-year segments and consider your work, home, social, educational, and recreational experiences in each segment. Choose the events that had the most meaning out of each segment (fig. 8.4).

Life Segment	Work	Family/Personal	Social/Recreation	Education
0–5		Mom-Dad	travel-cabin	
5–10				school—4th grade
10–15		brother died		pits
15–20	1st job—wards			
20–25	the bank	marriage	Europe	college
25–30	fired	ulcer		
30–35	manager	child		grad. school
35–40	vice-pres.	second child		
40–45	bored—sabbatical	marriage problems	marathon	
45–50		calm		teach part-time
50–55	second career	husband changes job, parents die		

Figure 8.4. Logical life image.

Complete the exercise by thinking of your life as if it were to be condensed into a feature article. What are the eight to ten peak events that had an impact on your life (either positively or negatively)? Times in which change occurred, you got a different image of yourself, or people influenced you in some way? What did you do at these times? Or chart out your life by drawing the most memorable turning points and listing their effects (fig. 8.5).

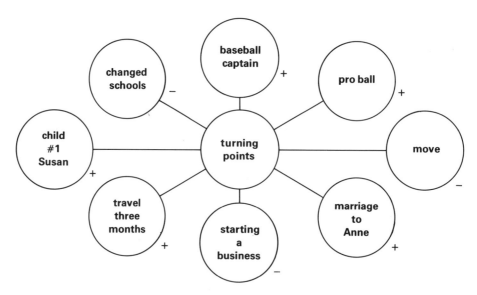

Figure 8.5.   Practical life image.

In the space below record the journey you have made in relation to the people, events, and experiences of your own life. If you need more space to record your life use a separate piece of paper.

Reflect on what you've learned about yourself from this life-cycle review exercise and share as much as you care to with a member of your inventure network. You may wonder what other people learned from this experience. Here are a few examples:

- A thirty-year-old woman saw marriage as her low point emotionally on her life-event line—twice. She realized that her life was being determined by men she chose to marry for the wrong reasons. She wanted to develop herself professionally and make the care of the children a shared experience. Both of her husbands wanted her to be a wife and mother only, in trade for financial security. She has determined now to consider *herself*, in addition to love, if she remarries.

- A forty-two-year-old male saw that each crisis in his life was followed by a positive experience. He decided to take more risks and "create crises" so he could create highs (move to a bigger city, ask for what he wanted, change jobs, travel without earning money first, hang glide).

- A fifty-year-old man found that all of his turning points involved close family members and social friends. Work had very little impact on his life. He decided to concentrate on lifestyle factors.

- A navy fighter pilot found that his life had been a series of distinct segments with abrupt endings. For instance, he was forced to retire at thirty-nine from an exciting, risky, and challenging life. He starts all over with each new segment, and is emotionally exhausted as a result.

- A twenty-six-year-old teacher found her life line to be perfectly flat until she finished school and had to support herself. She felt that she was experiencing life for the first time.

- A man at age fifty-five realized that three-quarters of his life was over. He'd never thought about it that way before. He decided to retire early and pursue his lucrative hobby.

Body

9

The body is the physical factor in the three life factors. Your body is your primary way of experiencing the world you live in. Just as the body of a boat that is well taken care of performs better, so too your body or physical well-being is essential. Inventurers realize that physical well-being is essential to the excursions they undertake. To consider new options, to venture and explore, requires optimum health and energy.

As John Gardner has stated, *"We are not at our best perched at the summit. We are climbers, at our best when the way is steep."*

For inventurers, the way is often steep, and that requires that we keep our bodies in optimum balance and efficiency with our minds and spirits. Physical well-being does not mean merely absence of illness or just physical appearance. It means achieving a state of health in which you are aware of and enjoy the very feel of your body and its rhythms. When we are liberated by a well-tuned body, we often stop watching life as spectators and start living life as actors. In this chapter we will consider energy patterns, stress on the body, physical relaxation, and visualization as key factors in the inventurous life.

ENERGY STYLE

Often, we experience an "energy crisis"—a human energy crisis—when we have to choose how to expend our energies during the 168 hours we have to live each week. We lament, "I wish there was more time to get everything done!" But that's it—168 hours is all!

How can you deal with the frustration of not having enough time to get things done? The first step is to be aware of the way you are using your energy. Our society has given very little attention to the importance of balance. Some of us have a work ethic which views a person who takes time off as being unproductive and lazy. Balance is needed even more today because of the pace of "present shock."

Energy styles are just emerging as an area of study. The problem at this point is figuring out the influence that energy has on our lives and what, if anything, we want to do about it.

Everyone's energy needs are different. Our energy patterns are determined primarily by social patterns: job, television schedules, family responsibilities. Some people feel best going to bed early, getting a full night's sleep, and awakening early in the morning. Others feel best if they sleep during the day and spend their waking hours at night. Some people attempt to conform to the eight-hour standard for sleep; others feel best with four to five hours. Everyone has a personal energy style, and it is helpful to be sensitive to it. Your body actually gives you messages, if you will listen. The amount of energy you have available for activities during a day and the amount of "recreation" you need will be highly individualized.

As a group, physical laborers are more in touch with their energy styles than are office workers, professional people, and homemakers. Fatigue in people who use their bodies in their work is more straightforward and easier to "read." Mental or nervous fatigue is more subtle and indirect. Mental and emotional efforts require as much energy as does physical work, but different parts of your body are doing the work. Complete the following exercises to learn more about your energy preferences.

Energy Expenditure

Rate your energy on the table below.

	1 Energy expenditure			2 Energy preferences		
Career	1	2	(3)	1	(2)	3
Friends	(1)	2	3	1	2	(3)
Social	1	(2)	3	1	(2)	3
Spouse/significant other	1	(2)	3	1	(2)	3
Children	1	2	3	1	2	3
Sports	(1)	2	3	1	2	(3)
Hobbies	(1)	2	3	1	(2)	3

	1 Energy expenditure			2 Energy preferences		
Self-growth	①	2	3	1	2	③
Community service	1	2	③	1	②	3
Personal time	①	2	3	1	2	③
Spirituality	①	2	3	1	2	③
Adventure	①	2	3	1	2	③

1. Rate yourself in column 1 on a continuum of 1–3, with 1 indicating a very low level of energy expenditure and 3 a very high level; e.g., "I think about my job all the time" ③ ; "I don't feel I spend enough time with my children" ① .

2. In column 2, rate your *preference*, the way you want to distribute your energy, with 3 being the person or activity you want to expend most energy on, and 1 the least. Are you comfortable with the way you are distributing energy now?

TRIGGERING EVENTS AND TENSION

We always wish we could do away with our tensions. You often hear, "If I just didn't have to work under so much pressure, I could relax and enjoy my life more, but the competition these days. . . ."

Jobs are never tense; people are. Coping with our self-induced tension is a vital skill. If we were completely free of all tension, we would no longer be alive. But there is positive tension and negative tension. Some tension is useful and productive; other tension gets in our way and inhibits us from performing as effectively as we might. There is not always a sharp dividing line between the positive and negative tensions. Too much negative tension can exact a physical as well as an emotional toll. Current research, pioneered by Dr. Hans Selye, a Canadian physician, links ailments such as ulcers, colitis, headaches, backaches, heart attacks, cancer, diabetes, and arthritis to stress. It also appears that chemical substances secreted into our bloodstreams in excess, when we are experiencing stress, have the effect of lowering our resistance to contagious or infectious illnesses. We are more likely to "catch" the flu or colds during a period of life stress than when the body's response to pressure is at a more positive level.

How much tension is too much? It depends on your ability to cope. Your answer is directly related to your evaluation of the forces or pressures influencing your behavior. Tension stems from within you—your reactions to external events.

How hard should I work? You'll have to answer another question first: "What do I want from my life?" But even that isn't the whole answer. The question "How hard should I work?" boils down to some fundamental choices about the way you want to live. How big a family, mortgage, or ego do you have to support?

Tension is a very real fact of life in our day-to-day activities. Each of us confronts the press of time, decision making, competition, and keeping up communications in relationships. In each case, it is not the "triggering event" itself that causes stress; rather, it is our response to that kind of situation. The vital element in coping with tension is the acceptance of the fact that no one outside of yourself can cause your tension. If you are tense, it's because you do it to yourself! Of course, there is a temptation to play "victim"—to feel that life would be much easier or that we would be much less tense if *they* would shape up. However, in any tension situation, you have two primary choices: (1) change the situation; or (2) change your mind set about the situation.

Triggering Events Rating Scale*

To change the situation, we must become aware of the specific events that are influencing our behavior; we must understand the source of our tension. Listed on page 68 are forty-three "triggering events," or "life events," which stimulate you to experience varying amounts of tension or stress. Check (✔) the specific events you have experienced in that past *two years*. If they've happened twice, put that number of points down twice. Then add points together to get your score.

150–199: Mild

200–299: Moderate

Over 300: Severe life crisis

For a two-year period, you are at risk, after a large total score. Thirty-three percent of the people with mild level scores developed some emotional or physical illness or problems, as did 48 percent of the moderates and 86 percent of those with scores over 300.

---

*Developed by T. H. Holmes and R. H. Rake, "The Social Readjustment Scale," *Journal of Psychosomatic Medicine* 2 (1967): 213. Reprinted by permission of Pergamon Press, Inc.

Life event	Stress level	My points
1. Death of spouse	100	
2. Divorce	73 ✓	
3. Marital separation	65	
4. Jail term	63	
5. Death of close family member	63	
6. Personal injury or illness	53	
7. Marriage	50	
8. Fired at work	47	
9. Marital reconciliation	45	
10. Retirement	45	
11. Change in health of family member	44	
12. Pregnancy	40	
13. Sex difficulties	39 ✓	
14. Gain of new family member	39	
15. Business readjustment	39 ✓	
16. Change in financial state	38 ✓	2
17. Death of close friend	37	39
18. Change to different line of work	36	31
19. Change in number of arguments with spouse	35	29
20. Mortgage over $30,000	31 ✓	26
21. Foreclosure of mortgage or loan	30	
22. Change in responsibilities at work	29 blah!	20
23. Son or daughter leaving home	29	12
24. Trouble with in-laws	29	157 Mild
25. Outstanding personal achievement	28 ✓	Jan '88?
26. Spouse beginning or stopping work	26	
27. Begin or end school	26	6
28. Change in living conditions	25 ✓	73
29. Revision of personal habits	24 ✓	39
30. Trouble with boss	23	39
31. Change in work hours or conditions	20	38
32. Change in residence	20	31
33. Change in schools	20	29
34. Change in recreation	19	28
35. Change in church activities	19	25
36. Change in social activities	18 ✓	24
37. Mortgage or loan less than $30,000	17	18
38. Change in sleeping habits	16	13
39. Change in number of family get-togethers	15	12
40. Change in eating habits	15	12/11/8
41. Vacation	13 ✓	369
42. Christmas, Chanuka	12 ✓	Severe Life crisis
43. Minor violations of the law	11	

My total points

RELAXATION

The second technique for reducing environmental tension is to change the mind that is dwelling on the situation. The ability to relax totally promotes mental alertness and allows you to act spontaneously and efficiently whenever "triggering events" require you to act. When you were small, the process of relaxing was easy. Since that time, you have been accumulating residual tensions, and you may be convinced that it's difficult for you to relax. It is very simple to relearn the process of relaxation. Think of it as getting back on your old bike. You may wobble a little at first, but you still remember how to use the pedals.

Tenseness occurs in different areas of our bodies. You might carry a large amount of tension in your neck, for example, whereas another person might carry tension in the stomach. Mental tension over "triggering events" is always manifested as physical tension in various parts of your body.

Your muscles are controlled by your mind. You can cause your muscles to completely relax. As you relax, you will find that it is easier for you to concentrate your attention in the direction you choose and to develop a much clearer perception of the events in your life. Try this ten-minute relaxation exercise.

Relaxation Exercise

1. Sit in a comfortable position. Consciously examine your physical tension and describe it to yourself in detail. Examine its intensity. Become as aware as you possibly can of the tension and related discomfort. Tense by tightening up the area; then relax it. If you touch the tense area with your hand, you will feel the discomfort. Interesting areas to try are your jaw, back, neck, and eye muscles. Most people are tense in these areas without being fully aware of it.

2. Close your eyes. Take several slow, deep breaths, breathing from your abdomen. Breathe in and out through your nose, taking breaths that are long and slow. Count "one" as you inhale and "two" as you exhale. Count your breaths over again with each breath cycle for five minutes. Concentrate on the numbers one and two, saying them to yourself with each breath cycle. The idea here is to clear your mind. Most of us feel controlled by the thoughts that constantly enter our minds. If you consider thoughts as they go through your mind, you realize you have stopped counting and started thinking. Visualize your thoughts as clouds floating toward you, floating freely into your mind, and then floating out of your mind again. Keep going back to counting your breaths. It will become easier as you practice.

3. Describe the effects this breathing has on your body. Do you feel less tense? Over a long period of time, you will definitely feel the effects of relaxation. (See the bibliography for further reading.)

VISUALIZATION

Visualization is one of the most powerful tools you have at your disposal. Researchers are discovering that our mind and the images within it can often determine career/life success or failure.

It has gone by many names throughout the years, including "the power of suggestion," "mind control," "meditation," and others. Almost every culture has in its own way stumbled upon this tool. Science is now adding evidence that these age-old traditions have a concrete basis in fact. Many religions, of course, have used the technique to assist people in achieving their spiritual goals.

So, not surprisingly, visualization—the process by which you can mentally picture your desired goal or results—is useful to career/life planning.

You're probably asking, "Can I (who has difficulty defining my career/life goals) picture options and transfer these to real life?" We believe the answer is, "Yes!" Visualization draws heavily upon modeling, a phenomenon common to most cultures of the world. Often language, customs, and other aspects of a culture are gradually learned through observing real-life models. In visualization you are simply creating your own models in your mind.

Doctors have known for a long time that some sick people can harness a great deal of energy to get better. Dr O. Carl Simonton, an oncologist, has adapted the visualization technique for his cancer patients, having them picture themselves as healthy, cancer-free individuals. In the business world, educational psychologist Steven DeVore has found that the characteristics of many "high achievers" include a trait he calls "sensory goal vision." These people seemed to know what they wanted out of life and could sense it before they ever had it. They could not only see it, but often could imagine the sounds, smells, and tastes associated with it. They envisioned it before they had it. And that vision became a driving force in their lives. Visualization colors our lives, and in many ways helps determine the kind of events that happen to us.

Relaxation plays an important role in visualization. In a relaxed state, your mind more easily adapts to picturing your options. Relaxation sets the stage properly. This initial condition is important. Once in a relaxed state you can tackle almost any challenge that needs work. Relaxation makes you more open to suggestion.

Visualization works best before breakfast or before dinner. The calming effect of the relaxed state can set a positive tone which may even last throughout the day or long into the evening. The least recommended time would be right after eating.

Visualization at least once a day is also recommended. It will make it easier for you to enter the relaxed state quickly and effortlessly. Now we come to the actual practice of visualization.

Career/Life Visualization Sequence

Step 1: Relaxing

There are many simple and effective methods to relax and narrow the focus of your conscious mind. The technique suggested earlier in this chapter is a good place to start.

Step 2: Deepening

Imagine yourself getting into your car, starting the engine, and beginning to drive. You leave the city or town in which you live and drive into whatever kind of rural setting would make you feel comfortable and relaxed. It might be a forest, a secluded beach, a mountain cabin, a garden, a sunny meadow—a real place, or totally made up. As your car gets near your destination, you begin to feel a deep tranquility, and a quiet comfort settles over you. You arrive feeling deeply peaceful, get out of the car, and enjoy being in your place. Just being there without doing anything gives you a soothing, nourishing feeling.

Step 3: Focusing

After you've enjoyed yourself in the quiet for a few moments, focus on a satisfying, successful, or ideal work situation:

- What are the surroundings like?
- What are you actually doing?
- What kinds of people are you doing it with (e.g., coworkers, clients)?
- What goals, purposes, or values are you trying to achieve?

Get as much clarity and focus of the situation as you can.

Step 4: Returning

Now reverse the deepening method step-by-step. Go back to your car. Drive back to the city. As you drive back, suggest to yourself that you are getting more and more alert—that you feel wonderful, refreshed, and quite awake when you return. Picture yourself feeling that way. Don't be in a big hurry to open your eyes. Returning faster than your natural rhythms would like can result in a less comfortable feeling. Experiment and find your proper rate.

This particular sequence can be modified in any way to suit your own individual needs. This is an extremely individual activity. No two people's visualization sequences should be the same.

VISUALIZING YOUR ENVIRONMENT

Creating an environment that expresses your vision of what you would like your lifestyle to be helps get you in harmony with your life and relieves tension. When you are at home or in a community or geographic situation that makes you ill at ease, tensions are created.

Living in life spaces you consciously choose maximizes harmony with your inner self, creating less tensions and more energy. What is your "vision" of the way things should be with your life spaces? Complete the following sequence.

My Life Space

1. Find a place that will be quiet and free of distractions for thirty minutes. Place a pencil and paper next to you. Find a comfortable position.

2. Complete the career/life visualization sequence. As you do this, keep in mind that some people will visualize their "life space," others will get a general feel for it, and still others will systematically list the elements of it. Any approach is fine.

   a) *Home space:* Imagine yourself in a living space (house, apartment, townhouse, etc.) where you feel perfectly at ease and happy. Imagine what the house is made of. Picture the furniture. Sit in a comfortable chair. What is it made of? How does it feel to your touch? Imagine the furnishings and decorations. What style do you picture? What colors surround you? Imagine little things around you—plants, rugs, artifacts, etc.

   b) *Geographic space:* Get up, walk to the back door, open it, and go outside. What is the landscape like around you? Water? Hills? Plains? Mountains? Trees? What is the climate like? Are there gardens, flowers, fields, forests? Walk two or three blocks away from your dwelling. Imagine the general landscape. Is there a neighborhood? Rural? City? Suburb? Foreign country? How large is the community? Is it a high-key (major city) or a low-key (small town) community? Imagine the people in the community. What do they look like? What are they doing? Or are you alone?

3. How do you feel right now? Relaxed? Tense? Highlight the life spaces you envisioned in your mind:

a) In the space provided write the ten most important things you considered in your life-space vision (e.g., house style, weather, rural, university access, etc.).

I "must" have:

1. _____
2. _____
3. _____
4. _____
5. _____
6. _____
7. _____
8. _____
9. _____
10. _____

I "want" to have:

1. _____
2. _____
3. _____
4. _____
5. _____
6. _____
7. _____
8. _____
9. _____
10. _____

b) In your ideal life space, which general area of the country or world did you envision yourself in?

c) Within the general location you selected in (b) above, select three places, cities, towns, or suburbs that might fit the specifications you designed in (a):

1. _____
2. _____
3. _____

d) How do your current life spaces compare with the information above?

4. You can start taking steps toward your ideal life spaces immediately. The effect can be gradual and cumulative (one small change per week, e.g., changing wall colors). That's more than fifty-two changes per year! Or, perhaps your life spaces require moving, building a house, changing geographic locations. Consider these immediate options:

a) Visit a nearby town, city, or neighborhood that most nearly resembles your ideal life space. Take pictures of life space areas similar to your goal. Visit with local people.

b) Subscribe to the newspaper in the area that epitomizes your ideal life space. Get a feel for the lifestyle tone—the issues, opportunities, and businesses that seem most important.

c) Visit your local library to obtain books that give further ideas about your ideal life space. Is there a publication that tends toward your interest? Ask your librarian.

d) Take a vacation in an area that resembles your ideal life space. Write the questions you want answered and the people you want to see. Write the Chamber of Commerce for suggestions.

The main point is to provide life spaces where you can relax and be free of tensions imposed by an environment you do not like.

 Enter your preferred life space location (3.c) on your excursion map (Box 7).

Mind

10

The mind is the intellectual life factor. When you think of things you've learned in school, you usually think of activities in this area: communication, thinking, learning, writing, organizing, and creating. A great deal of time is spent concentrating on excellence in this area all through our early years.

Some interesting research is under way in the mind area, studying the different usages of parts of the human brain. There are some exciting discoveries connecting our right brain with our creativity, visual perception, cyclical thought, invention, intuition, nontechnical knowledge, and holistic learning. We are just beginning to tap the capacity of the human brain—the 95 percent we don't use. The most exciting discoveries are yet to come based on the early work of Jung, Bruner, James, Ornstein, and Bogen.

THE RIGHT AND LEFT BRAINS

In this chapter we would like to introduce you to your right brain in a way that will be fun and persuasive as well. We are borrowing these summaries and exercises from a wonderful book by Betty Edwards, called *Drawing on the Right Side of the Brain.*

Most of us are afraid to draw anything. We think back to our first representations of houses, the sun, flowers, and children with amusement, but when asked to draw the same scenes now, we shriek, "All I can draw are stick figures." We've become stuck, largely because of messages from our left brain, as we shall see in a minute (see fig. 10.1).

Now you're asking, "But what does drawing have to do with the two sides of the brain?" To oversimplify the explanation, the two brain halves,

Figure 10.1. Child's drawing.

right and left, serve different functions quite opposite from each other. According to our current understanding, we need both the left brain or mode of consciousness, and the right brain or mode of consciousness. We use both, but many of us are less accustomed to using the right mode, the intuitive one. It is helpful to tap the right brain in order to draw likeness and to make connections that take us beyond stick figures. Learning to draw is also a good way for those of us left-brain-oriented people to experience what the right brain can do. After learning to draw, we can translate the experience to everyday problems as well. In fact, most of this book is an attempt to get you to do life and career planning with both sides of your brain. Keep that in mind as you complete the book. Before we experiment with drawing (relax, it'll be fun), these are the descriptions of the two brains or modes of consciousness.

A Comparison of Left-Mode and Right-Mode Characteristics

L MODE

Verbal: Using words to name, describe, define.

Analytic: Figuring things out step-by-step and part-by-part.

R MODE

Nonverbal: Awareness of things, but minimal connection with words.

Synthetic: Putting things together to form wholes.

Symbolic: Using a symbol to *stand for* something. For example, the drawn form 👁 stands for *eye*, the sign + stands for the process of addition.	Concrete: Relating to things as they are, at the present moment.
Abstract: Taking out a small bit of information and using it to represent the whole thing.	Analogic: Seeing likenesses between things; understanding metaphoric relationships.
Temporal: Keeping track of time, sequencing one thing after another: Doing first things first, second things second, etc.	Nontemporal: Without a sense of time.
Rational: Drawing conclusions based on *reason* and *facts*.	Nonrational: Not requiring a basis of reason or facts; willingness to suspend judgment.
Digital: Using numbers as in counting.	Spatial: Seeing where things are in relation to other things, and how parts go together to form a whole.
Logical: Drawing conclusions based on logic: one thing following another in logical order—for example, a mathematical theorem or a well-stated argument.	Intuitive: Making leaps of insight, often based on incomplete patterns, hunches, feelings, or visual images.
Linear: Thinking in terms of linked ideas, one thought directly following another, often leading to a convergent conclusion.	Holistic: Seeing whole things all at once; perceiving the overall patterns and structures, often leading to divergent conclusions.

Figure 10.2. A comparison of left-mode and right-mode characteristics.[*]

One of the most graphic examples of the differences between the right and the left brains in drawing is portrayed in Edwards's book: the Picasso drawing exercise. You are simply to look at one of Picasso's famous drawings (of Igor Stravinsky) and draw it as you see it, only looking at it upside down. The reason for this is that when we look at things right side up we name and categorize them and block our right brains. We don't see shapes but rather legs, arms, etc. When we turn the thing upside down, we see shadow, different shapes, new relationships, and angles. If you are wondering about this, just write your signature below, turn the book upside down, and see how different it looks to you.

Signature: _____

Take a deep breath and try this exercise in drawing, even if stick figures were your last attempt. Look at the upside-down Picasso drawing on page 78 and draw it upside down according to the directions.

Just to show you that we're good sports, and that we too discovered something, Janet's Picasso rendition is shown on page 78.

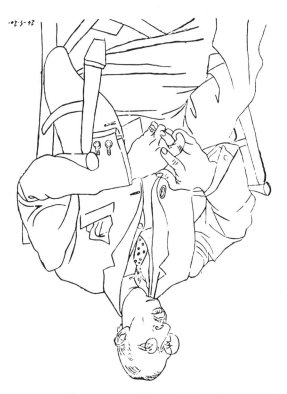

Figure 10.3   Picasso's Drawing

Janet's Picasso

Before you begin: Read all of the following instructions.

1. Find a quiet place to draw where no one will interrupt you. Play music if you like. As you shift into R-mode, you may find that the music fades out. Finish the drawing in one sitting, allowing yourself about thirty to forty minutes—more if possible. Set an alarm clock or a timer, if you wish, so that you can forget about keeping time (an L-mode function). And more importantly: *do not turn the drawing right side up until you have finished.* Turning the drawing would cause a shift back to L-mode, which we want to avoid while you are learning to experience the R-mode.

2. Look at the upside-down drawing (Figure 10.3) for a minute. Regard the angles and shapes and lines. You can see that the lines all *fit* together. Where one line ends another starts. The lines lie at certain angles in relation to each other and in relation to the edges of the paper. Curved lines fit into certain spaces. The lines, in fact, form the edges of space, and you can look at the shapes of the spaces within the lines.

3. When you start your drawing, begin at the top and copy each line, moving from line to adjacent line, putting it all together just like a jigsaw puzzle. Don't concern yourself with naming the parts; it's not necessary. In fact, if you come to parts that perhaps you *could name*, such as the H-A-N-D-S or the F-A-C-E (remember, we are not *naming things!*), just continue to think to yourself, "Well, this line curves that way; this line crosses over, making that little shape there; this line is at that angle, compared to the edge of the paper," and so on. Again, try not to think about what the forms are and avoid any attempt to recognize or name the various parts.

4. Begin your upside-down drawing now, working your way through the drawing by moving from line to line, part to adjacent part.

5. Once you've started drawing, you'll find yourself becoming very interested in how the lines go together. By the time you are well into the drawing, your L-mode will have turned off (this is not the kind of task the left hemisphere readily takes to: it's too slow and it's too hard to recognize anything), and your R-mode will have turned on.

Remember that everything you need to know in order to draw the image is *right in front of your eyes.* All of the information is right there, making it easy for you. Don't make it complicated. It really is as simple as that.

Spirit

11

The emotional life element is by far the most elusive one. Social scientists have been trying for years to understand, teach, and evaluate the emotional, or affective, sides of us. The field of counseling strives to help people understand how this area affects their actions. When asked to list all the feelings they could think of, one group of people listed over 100 different feelings! But feelings are just part of this life element. Your sense of self-identity, relationships with others and your environment, values and attitudes, and religious or spiritual beliefs are also included. Together, these components make up your life "code"—your philosophy of life.

There is evidence emerging that people who have developed an integrated life "code," or consistent set of beliefs and actions, tend to manage their tension better. The process of life and career renewal, if taken seriously, could become part of your life code. It is a process to help you actualize your beliefs. In this chapter, we will focus on three major areas—your self-image, your values and life issues, together making up your broad life purpose. Use your imagination, your innermost reactions, your subconscious fantasies when learning about your spirit. It emerges more and more as you give it time and permission. Many people are fearful of their spiritual side, and do not know how interwoven it is in their life codes.

YOUR SELF-IMAGE
What Are My Strengths?

We hear people say again and again, "Oh, I can't serve on that committee. I'm not well organized." Or, "I really wonder how far I'll go because I'm not really very bright." Or, "How can I manage people if I haven't had psychology?" We are much more prone to putting ourselves down than to building ourselves up. If we do feel or say good things about ourselves, we think we're bragging. There is a fine line sometimes between humility, pride, and honest self-esteem. It is a lifelong process for most of us just to build our basic self-esteem and at the same time not let our egos control us.

The point is that we are all strong in some qualities or characteristics and weak in others. But we think the really good characteristics, the most valued ones, are not the ones we possess. It's time we all begin to recognize our best traits and then find ways to use them most effectively.

Personal Qualities

As you can see below, there are several stacks of cubes labeled as different personal qualities. These are not all the qualities available, but represent a sampling of the range of qualities. Get ready to be very honest with yourself, to not underestimate yourself. You may need to get feedback from others on this exercise, just to act as a check on your own thinking.

1. Look at all the quality cubes and put a star (*) above the one you admire most.

2. Think now about your own qualities and how you would "stack up" against the general population. Shade in the cubes up to the level at which you see yourself. You can use the statements, "I see myself at the level in comparison to other people." We are all high in one or more of these qualities listed. You can use specific groups to compare yourself to after you have completed the first round—like friends, women, men, or work associates. Just use different colors and draw vertical lines next to the boxes instead of coloring them in.

For instance, Jane sees herself this way generally,

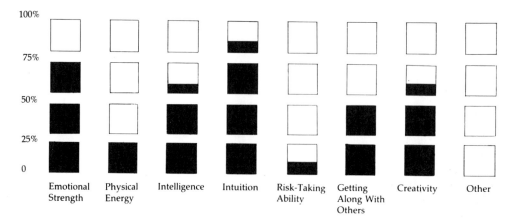

and this way when compared to the people she works with.

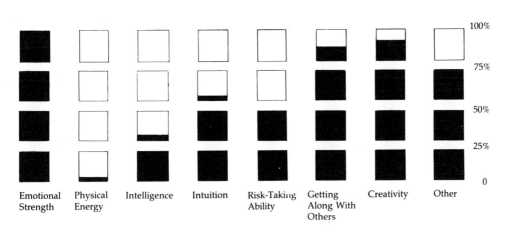

Emotional Strength | Physical Energy | Intelligence | Intuition | Risk-Taking Ability | Getting Along With Others | Creativity | Other

Personality Quality Cubes

How Do You Stack Up?

3. I see myself at the highest level (_____%) in comparison to people generally in the quality of _____.

What are my other, highest qualities?

_____, _____, _____

4. Which quality (of all qualities) do I admire the most in others? _____
_____. Why? _____
_____
_____

5. If the quality you admired most is not one of your mid- to high-range qualities, can you still value highly your own qualities while admiring the qualities of others? _____. If not, why not? _____
_____
_____

Enter your 3 best, highest qualities on your excursion map (Box 8).

Broad Life Code

Look back at the Life-Cycle Review Exercise using the excursion model (fig. 8.1, p. 59). Think about what matters most in your life, what you prize or value. Is it a good job, people, risk taking, travel, children, security, health? You can tell by the consistent way in which these issues are related to your life events; e.g., every low had to do with illness, or every good decision had to do with personal growth and freedom.

Not all of your values will be reflected in your life events, so we'll give you a chance to look a little more globally at your values. Unlike the last exercise in which we asked what your actual personal qualities are, we are asking you what you believe in or value the most.

1. Read through the list of life values and rank those values that are reflected by life events or other behavior you consistently show in your life: 1 is high, 20 is low. Don't check what you think you *should* value (e.g., my work), but check what your behavior *shows*. Use the question, "If I were to give up the values one at a time, which would go first, which last?" The last to go is your highest value, #1.

Others' values	My values	
( )	( )	Achievement (sense of accomplishment/promotion)
( )	( )	Adventure (exploration, risks, excitement)
( )	( )	Personal freedom (independence, making own choices)
( )	( )	Authenticity (being frank and genuinely yourself)
( )	( )	Expertness (being good at something important to me)
( )	( )	Emotional health (ability to handle inner feelings)
( )	( )	Service (contribute to satisfaction of others)
( )	( )	Leadership (having influence and authority)
( )	( )	Money (plenty of money for things I want)
( )	( )	Spirituality (meaning to life, religious belief)
( )	( )	Physical health (attractiveness and vitality)
( )	( )	Meaningful work (relevant and purposeful job)
( )	( )	Affection (warmth, caring, giving and receiving love)
( )	( )	Pleasure (enjoyment, satisfaction, fun)
( )	( )	Wisdom (mature understanding, insight)
( )	( )	Family (happy and contented living situation)
( )	( )	Recognition (being well known, praised for contribution)

Others' values	My values	
( )	( )	Security (having a secure and stable future)
( )	( )	Self-growth (continuing exploration and development)
( )	( )	Mental health (having a keen, active mind)

2. Compare your ranking with that of a special person in your life. Use the column marked "Others' values." How are they alike? Different?

3. Now go back and choose the top three that you consider most important for the future. They may be different from your highest ranked values. Which value do you consider #1, 2, 3?

   1 _____

   2 _____

   3 _____

4. Are your values more oriented to mind, body, or spirit? For instance, do you value the physical, intellectual, or emotional realm? Which life factor is most prominent overall? _____Mind _____Body _____Spirit

You will see shortly how values and personal qualities fit into one's life purpose, but first we need to have you address your life issues.

Enter your top values on the excursion map (Box 9).

LIFE ISSUES

In the last few years, we have found that more and more people are reflecting about their lives and thinking more seriously about what it all means to them. Usually this occurs at midlife or later. We think it can occur much sooner. This exercise is intended to rouse you to think about the unstated (or stated) issues in your life that you are solving or hope to solve in the future. You may be surprised or disappointed with what you find out because you hadn't thought about issues much before. There is always time to begin now.

What are some issues in our lives and how can we tell one when we see one? Let's answer the second question first. Your life issues are represented by the ways in which you spend your only resources—time, energy, and money. Answer the following questions and see what it tells you.

How do you spend your nonwork time? (home? community?)

What volunteer organizations do you work with? Why?

In what organizations have you been a leader? Why?

Do your involvements serve a larger issue in the society? What issue?

What contributions do you make? Why?

Are your involvements helpful or harmful to other people? How?

If you had one-quarter of your time free to devote to an issue, what would you choose?

Your answers to these questions ought to tell you whether or not you have thought about life issues, whether you have identified some, and whether you have made a commitment to work on any. Some people have no issues they can identify. Others may have learned that your major issue is yourself at the expense of others, or others like family, at the expense of yourself.

There are times in our lives when we pull back from outside activities and times we move into them. This may be dependent on our life stage. The important thing is to think about what you're involved in and why, so it reflects the issues of concern to you. One committed person is worth five who are lukewarm.

Look back over your answers to the questions and decide which issues your involvements represent. For instance, if you are involved in cancer research activities, then health may be your issue, or if you are involved with a battered women's shelter, then the problems of relationships or women's safety may be your issue, or if you are involved in nothing, then. . . .
Here are a sampling of issues that other people have listed:

Problems of the poor	Public TV	Women and money	Housing
Family strength	Sports promotion	Health	Unemployment
Political change	Aging populations	Spirituality	Good government
The arts	Hunger	Minority businesses	Work ethic
Protection of women's safety	Meaningful leisure	Education	Youth development

Acquisition of   World peace   Legal rights   Self
wealth
Alcoholism

What issues are strong in your life?

Are you satisfied? If not, what changes do you intend to make? When?

 Enter your main life issue(s) on the Excursion map (Box 10).

LIFE PURPOSE

Together the three factors of personal qualities, values, and life issues make up your life purpose. Your purpose is the qualities you offer to further issues you care about consistent with values you hold. We add one more dimension, activity, to tell you *what* you will do.

Now remember, we said that not everyone has a stated life purpose. Many of us haven't even thought about our purpose, while others have several purposes. Many people feel they are led to a purpose through a spiritual experience. Some of us are having a "crisis of purpose." Some of us have lost our purpose and are looking for a new one. Many of us fell into ours through someone else or by a strange coincidence, an unexpected event. Whatever your situation, this whole section on the spirit is designed to get you thinking about purpose because we believe that people with a purpose are more satisfied, more clear in their direction, even happier sometimes. They are inventurers.

Here are some examples of statements of life purposes:

- I use my <u>creativity</u> and leadership to do P.R. for a <u>neighborhood housing</u>
        (quality)   (activity)   (issue)
  <u>group</u>.

- Because I value <u>family life</u> and hate to see <u>children alone at home</u>, I
            (value)   (issue)

organized and now run a <u>co-op after school activity</u> room in our neigh-
  (quality)   (activity)
borhood.

- There is <u>no theater</u> in this town. I will <u>use my influence</u> by <u>designing a</u>
           (issue)   (quality)
  <u>master plan</u> to <u>present</u> to the business association. It would <u>bring in new</u>
  (activity)   (activity)
  <u>business</u> and also be <u>enjoyable</u>.
            (value)

Of course, they can be much more simply stated as well, as long as they are carefully thought through.

- I'm going to work on hunger in our city.
- I'll get on the education committee at church.
- I'm ready to run for office.

What is your life purpose at this point in your life?

Enter your life purpose on your excursion map (Box 11).

The Rebalancing Act

12

It is no small task to summarize lifestyles and life factors or to consider the balance of these factors in your life. Now that you have a broader perspective on your lifestyle, how would you change your three life factors in size? Maybe you confirmed what you thought. Or perhaps you are even more out of balance than you thought. Perhaps at this point in your life you'd like to be *more* out of balance, to expand the size of one of the life factors!

   Here are some examples of ways in which you can expand each of your life factors—body, mind, and spirit.

Body	*Mind*	*Spirit*
exercise	change mind set	the arts
nutrition-diet	creativity	belief system
rest	listening—people,	confirmed
relaxation	music	relationships with
physical hobbies with	get task done	others
hands	journal writing	focus on sensitivity to
sports, dance	work out options	others, community
meditation	self-analysis	change attitude
physical exam	therapy	toward self/others
grooming	study-school	spirituality
physical image change	be alone with	psychic awareness
driving	thoughts	humor
physical risks	games of the mind	nature

sleep
travel

reading
imagery-dreams
research project
intellectual hobbies

cultivate happy
    people
risk beyond self
music

In the space below, redraw your life factors (see fig. 7.1, p. 53) according to the percentage of time, interest, and activity *you want them* to take in your life. Compare them with your first life-factors drawing.

Your Lifestyle Summary

Answer the following questions to conclude the lifestyle section:

1. Are you satisfied with yourself as a result of the information you gained or confirmed about your lifestyle? Yes _____ No _____

2. If yes, go on to Section IV. (You may want to complete the Life Goals Exercise anyway!)

3. If no, *stop* here and decide what you want to do differently, now and in the future. Complete the Life Goals Exercise and the Excursion Contract Exercise and concentrate on fulfilling some of your goals before proceeding to the work-style section.

Life Goals

It's crucial that you consider what you'd *like* to do with your lifestyle factors in the future—that is, if you want more satisfaction and balance. We're going to assist you by giving you a chance to dream again. Pick up your pen and in the next ten minutes (time yourself), write in the space below all the things you want to achieve in relation to the following factors before you die. *Be specific*, e.g., live in the mountains, run six miles a day, stay home with the children full time, lose weight. Get ready, get set, GO.

Personal (health, fitness, travel, hobbies, schooling, personal growth, travel, adventures, etc.) _____

_____

_____

_____

Career/work (career changes, positions, second careers, earnings, special projects, new skills, credentials, etc.) _____

_____

_____

_____

_____

Relationships (family activities, marriage enrichment, friendships, mentors, etc.) _____

_____

_____

_____

Spiritual (spiritual growth, community service, church activities, problems you're interested in solving, people you're interested in helping, etc.) ____

_____

_____

_____

Lifestyle (type of living situations, geographic locale, complexity or simplicity of living, time allocation, life balance, etc.) _____

_____

_____

_____

Other _____

_____

_____

STOP!

1. Now pick the *top three* short-term goals you selected and mark them with an *.

2. Next, give each of the three a priority. Which is most important, second, and third? You must make the choice; that's part of the process.

Write your #1 lifestyle goal here, and enter it on your excursion map (Box 12).

One way of clarifying how valued a goal is for you is to ask:

1. Am I ready to make a written commitment to that goal?
2. Am I setting a deadline?
3. Is it based on my values?
4. Can I visualize it in considerable detail?

Remember, you can eat an elephant only one bite at a time. Achieving long-term goals is difficult unless you start with the smallest step. But you must start on the first step, or you'll wake up at age seventy with nothing but regrets and excuses. We invite you to write your lifestyle goal on the Excursion Contract on page 92 and fill in the information, sharing it with someone who can support your achievement.

Excursion Contract

Goal: What do I want to accomplish? Result expected?

_____

_____

_____

Resources I can use: Action steps   *Target dates*

1. _____   1. _____

2. _____   2. _____

3. _____   3. _____

4. _____   4. _____

5. _____   5. _____

Obstacles: What are my favorite obstacles that I let get in the way (time, money, other people, self-image, experience, etc.)?

_____

_____

_____

_____

Reward: What do I get when I finish?

_____

_____

_____

Penalty: What if I don't finish?

_____

_____

_____

_____   _____
Completion date   My signature

                                         _____
                                         My partner's signature

Work Styles

IV

Making a Living Work

13

Work—and the perception of work—are going through some redefinitions. For all our age-old preoccupation with work, we have not as yet been able to come up with a very satisfactory definition of it. Kahlil Gibran defined work as *"love made visible."* People work for a wide variety of reasons and get various rewards from their efforts. Work is a paradox. We work when we are hungry, and it is obvious that we also work when we are well fed, well clothed, and well housed. We typically devote nearly half of our waking hours to work.

When we devote significant amounts of time to anything, we are implicitly assuming that it is important to do so. Some of us work hard at making a living. Inventurers are seeking ways to "make a living work" for them. They are seeking "good work" as opposed to a "good job."

What are the growing numbers of people who are seeking "good work" trying to find? Good work and a good job are not the same thing. A good job is often defined as clean, high-paying, secure, and prestigious. Good work is different. Good work is often defined as "integrated"—something in which who you are and what you do fit together congruently. Or more specifically, good work includes a harmonious coordination of experience, interests, skills, and conscience—balance of mind, body, and spirit. Like a patchwork quilt with the separate pieces woven together, good work allows us to blend work activities that fit with our values, goals, skills, and interests, or as George Bernard Shaw stated, *"to be able to choose the line of greatest advantage instead of yielding in the path of least resistance. . . ."* In our quest for good work, we "choose the line of greatest advantage" because we see work in the total context of our lives and understand that we do our best work in those areas in which we are most interested and that fit our abilities.

Work is a paradox. It helps us live with ourselves in many ways. People often say, "I'd go nuts if I didn't work." On the other hand, work often makes it difficult to live with ourselves. A young service station attendant explained his observations this way:

- "If they come into the station in the morning, they can still be friendly and act like they're human. But if the same people stop on their way home, watch out! They either just stare straight ahead through their windshields while I fill the tank, or they seem like they're just looking for ways to take it out on me! That's why I try to work weekends."

According to repeated studies, we do not choose to free ourselves from work even if we have a chance. Our own study of a major corporation asked 1500 employees (surveyed from top to bottom), "If you had enough money to live comfortably for the rest of your life, would you continue to work?" Take a minute to answer that question yourself.

Seventy percent in this survey said they would! However, of that 70 percent, 60 percent indicated that they would try to find "good work"—different from a good job. Of course, they all defined good work differently. But the point is that working, and particularly at a *meaningful* type of work, was something most people would voluntarily seek and choose to do. And their definitions of good work were fascinating! It was almost as if they had never thought what working meant to them, but now that they were presented with the "removal" of it, they were able to express feelings which had been there implicitly all the time.

Nearly all of us derive some sense of usefulness and worth from working. Our egos are often so bound up in our jobs that if we were not working (i.e., were laid off or retired), our feelings of insignificance might even lead to emotional and physical problems. As the old adage says: *"To work is to live, and those who do not work seem to die."* This literally becomes the case with some people who die shortly after retirement. We usually choose work over idleness, even if we have enough money to live well without working.

Work has many meanings for us:

1. *Personal identity:* When we work, we have a contributing place in society. We feel that we earn the right to be the partner of other people—we earn our membership in society. The fact that someone will pay us for our work is often an indication that what we do is needed by others, and therefore, we matter—as individuals. In fact, this is so important that in our study, outlined above, *40 percent* of the people who would choose to work would choose a line of work in which they could make a significant contribution to others, work that would give their lives meaning and purpose. Work is a major social

device for our identification as adults. "Who we are" is directly interwoven with "what we do."

2. *Relationships:* When we work, we have a reason to be with others. Most work activity requires interaction and communication. It's not uncommon for people to indicate that they would miss the socializing aspects of their work *most* if they retired or did not work. It is not unusual also to find people who live lonely lives after working hours, particularly those people who do not make friends easily. In fact, people often speak of their organization as being a "family."

3. *Money:* Realistically, most people need to provide financially for themselves and to protect themselves against possible emergencies as well as the realities of aging. Work has a fundamental economic meaning as a medium for survival. However, there comes a time when money ceases to be our main work motivator. Money is an important incentive to some, not for fundamental financial needs, but because of its symbolic importance. Its acquisition symbolizes for many people power, achievement, success, recognition, and many other things. Sometimes we justify our work by aspiring to a certain position in life, to "arrive." Often our justification is more truly a matter of trying to be loved, through symbolic recognition or prestige.

In recent years studies of motivation to work frequently have emphasized a variety of important work meanings. Psychologist Abraham Maslow theorized that needs are the primary influences on our behavior. When a particular need emerges in us, it determines our motivations, priorities, and actions. Motivated behavior is the result of the tension—pleasant or unpleasant—experienced when a need emerges. Our actions reduce this tension. Thus unsatisfied needs are our primary motivators to get us to act. Maslow developed five levels of needs and arranged them on an ascending pyramid (fig. 13.1).

When we satisfy our needs at one level of the pyramid, we move next to satisfy our new needs at the level immediately above that. Like a hiker going up a mountain, we are continually seeking to reach the top of the pyramid. A storm may come along and send us scurrying back down for safety, food, and shelter at the base of the pyramid. But as those needs are met, we again begin the ascent.

Our work-related needs can be divided into three levels:

1. *"Having" needs:* The basic needs for food, shelter, and clothing are met in most "jobs." "Just a job," a phrase often heard, satisfies our basic-level (having) needs of life by providing the money to purchase material goods, food, housing, and clothing. How much of your paycheck do you spend just to maintain your lifestyle spending patterns? Does money represent a game, a challenge, to you?

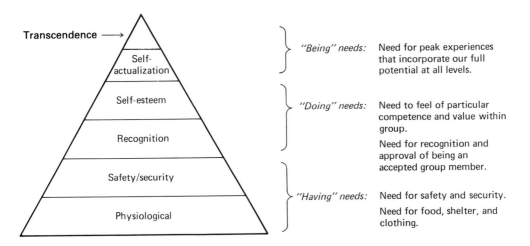

Fig. 13.1. Maslow's hierarchy of needs.

2. *"Doing" needs:* The need to accomplish something, do something well, and be recognized for it often comes through success or competence in a chosen vocation. It is more than "just a job." Perhaps we are working in a particular field, for a special idea, or for a particular organization or leader. As people work their way up an organization or as they get older, these doing needs seem more prevalent. In what kinds of work situations would you work harder than you ordinarily do, putting out more energy and enthusiasm because you felt the work deserved it?

3. *"Being" needs:* These needs arise when we desire more personal fulfillment. We may want to make a more lasting impact. We may feel a sense of mission or cause on an issue we identify with. There is a need to experience a spiritual, intellectual, or aesthetic dimension, a more fulfilling "quality of life." Often our spare time or leisure interests might reflect this need. If you could use your work to indulge in your favorite form of interest or play, what would you be doing?

Visualizing this, some of us are fortunate enough to have all five need areas met through our work situations. Others of us might get one or two needs met. And some of us might experience the higher levels of need satisfaction through aspects of our lives other than work (e.g., church, family, hobbies, professional groups). (See fig. 13.2.)

Some of us make work out of play, and some of us make play out of work. Why do you work? What's your definition of "good work"? Being aware of your own needs and priorities is an important aspect of your own excursion process.

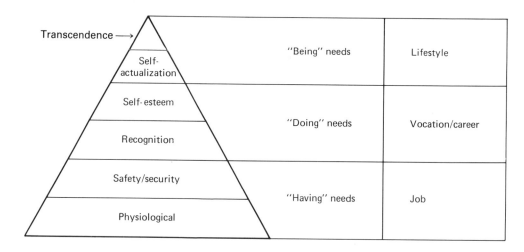

Figure 13.2.   Integration of needs and activities.

Why Do I Work?

Directions: Consider the following fourteen work-related needs. In column A, *rank* your work-value preferences from 1–14 in order of importance to you. By the end of the exercise, you should be able to say, "I need _____ more than _____, and _____ more than _____," etc. Think of your needs in terms of the work setting rather than overall personal needs.

Have you experienced your work-value preferences in any previous jobs or work activities? Write at the top of columns B, C, and D the titles or key words for work activities or jobs you've had in the past few years, including present work. Rank the values *that were present* in each activity or job.

	A	B	C	D
Recognition and approval (self and work known and others)				
Variety (new and different things)				
Socioeconomic status (meet standards with respect to material matters)				
Dependence (work guided by others)				
Economic security (assurance of continuing income)				
Interpersonal relations (acceptance and belongingness with other people)				

	A	B	C	D
Mastery, skill, and achievement (do a task well according to one's own standards)				
Independence (direct one's own behavior)				
Service and social welfare (have one's efforts result in benefits to others)				
Leadership and personal power (direct and have influence over others)				
Creativity and challenge (meet new problems, produce new and original work)				
Adventure (situations with risk and change)				
Self-expression (behavior consistent with self-concept)				
Moral value (behavior consistent with moral code)				

Compare your preferences (column A) with your work experiences (columns B, C, and D). Answer the following questions:

1. In my present work, I need more _____, _____, and _____. I'm getting enough _____ and _____.

2. My present job's work values and reward structures show that what I do is worth spending part of my life on. _____ Yes _____ No

   Comment: _____

   _____

   _____

3. My future work will require _____, and _____.

   _____

4. My idea of "good work" is _____.

5. On the Maslow hierarchy, my values reflect strongest _____ having, _____ doing, or _____ being needs.

   Enter your top three work-value preferences on the excursion map (Box 13).

HOW HARD SHOULD I WORK?

The exercise above begs yet another important question: How hard should I work? Although this question was addressed in the section on lifestyle, it is important enough to consider again briefly.

Many of us suffer from a basic malady: an unhealthy, yet compelling attachment to work. We put in fifty-five- to one-hundred-hour weeks and rarely take vacations. We always have "too much to do and not enough time to do it," and we keep our body stress levels high around the clock trying to get it all done. Again, we see the paradox of work. Work is viewed as a virtue on the one hand. But taken to its extreme, work is viewed as a malady—"workaholism."

Workaholism often undermines productivity and creativity—the very reasons given for working extra-long hours. By failing to "recreate," workaholics frequently turn out work of less quality and quantity than if they had taken time to recharge their batteries.

We are born of the "Puritan work ethic," which consistently traces itself back through history. The fact that dedicated nose-to-the-grindstone activity is almost universally admired, honored, and rewarded in our society makes it even more difficult for some of us to ask, "How hard *should* I work?" Hard work, even though often creating severe lifestyle imbalances, masquerades as a virtue in our society. It's not necessarily bad to work hard at a job that you enjoy or that is challenging. But the true workaholic is likely to pay a heavy price in health, family life, leisure enjoyment, spiritual and emotional development, and even career advancement, despite the seeming benefits of dedication to the job. The reason is obvious—the "postponed life." The qualities of life and living that demand time and energy to flower must be postponed or denied. Most workaholics don't deliberately intend to forfeit these human needs; they just "never get around to them!" It is always tomorrow that the workaholic plans to slow down, enjoy, savor, experience new things. But tomorrow rarely comes.

Some workaholics are frightened that they will fail to perform well, that someone above them will decide they don't measure up, or that they will fall behind and be forgotten. Workaholics are often victims of a set of beliefs, however acquired, that they must "be perfect"—constantly performing well, without any mistakes. Often personal identity and self-worth come solely from work and its universal scorecard, money.

The $corecard

14

Money. Think about it. Money is the most often discussed yet least understood commodity in our society. Unfortunately, it is the "$corecard" for the game of living—the scorecard for self-esteem in our society. In fact, most social and work gatherings inevitably drift back to discussing money. "How much are they worth?" "What did they pay for that?" Along with the weather, discourse about money has become a national pastime. Money is the "most talked about game in town."

Yet for all our preoccupation with money, we know very little about how and why money affects us. Of course, we all know the standard folklore about money which has endured, largely unquestioned, since the beginning of the Industrial Revolution:

- "A penny saved is a penny earned."
- "If it's worth doing, it's worth doing well."
- "Waste not, want not."
- "Penny wise, pound foolish."
- "Idle hands are a devil's workshop."
- "Never put off until tomorrow what you can do today."
- "Work before play."

These quotes reflect values stressing thrift and work. Accordingly, productivity and money are supposed to be the main motives, if not the only ones, that most people have for working.

Of course, work has a fundamental economic meaning as a medium for survival. The need for money is a basic, but rarely the only, reason for working. And when people are able to earn enough to meet their fundamental "having" needs, other needs become proportionately more important to them.

Numerous studies have shown that when supervisors are asked to rate the factors that motivate their subordinates, money is nearly always at or near the top of the list. When the people themselves are asked to rate their own motives, however, money is usually ranked below such factors as job security, job interest, and agreeable coworkers. The question "Who is right?" is neither answerable nor important. Both groups are reporting the reality they choose to see. How did you rank money (i.e., socioeconomic status and economic security) on the exercise on p. 104.

It seems that many of us intend to enjoy the good life through financial independence, but very few of us ever achieve it. According to insurance company studies, of every hundred people born in the United States, only *ten* are alive and have an independent income at age sixty-five. What has happened to the other ninety? Thirty-six are dead before sixty-five, and fifty-four more are broke, eking out their retirement years on social security and maybe a pension, or worse, by support from relatives or welfare payments.

From these statistics, our financial probabilities seem like the odds in a card game. There is an important difference, however. In cards, you at least know the rules of the game when you sit down to play. You also know that you can drop out whenever you please. We can't always drop out of the money game as easily. ("Responsibilities, you know!") We often don't even consider our odds, or define our reasons, for playing the money game—perhaps because we don't dare! If we care to learn about the odds, however, we can play the game better. And if we don't like the odds, *we can change the game.*

We must not discount the importance of money. It is a complex influencing factor in many areas. Money takes on "scorecard" meanings for many people. In addition to being a medium of exchange, its supposed purpose, it becomes a symbol of other values. To some people, money represents social respectability; to others, recognition for achievement; to still others, worldliness, materialism, and the "root of all evil." Since money *can* represent the "scorecard" in our lives, we must at least define the rules in the game we're going to play.

The money game is one of continuous action. Satisfaction from money comes usually from an *increasing* income, not from income itself. We are continuously keeping score! We often feel that our current income is something we have already earned, rather than something to be appreciated. When's the last time, after a salary increase, that you said to yourself, "This is great. I'm really going to put out this year for dear old XYZ organization." We spend more time being dissatisfied with our incomes than being satisfied. Why is this?

One explanation for keeping continuous score is the notion pursued by advertising and marketing strategists that we have an insatiable appetite for upgrading our standard of living. We focus our attention on the visible "scorecard" rather than on the invisible reality of our lives. When we're insecure, we seek money to make us secure again. We try to make more money, buy clothes, etc., to bolster our sagging self-images. Satisfaction is sought through the tangible "scorecard"—money. When we want to make a career or lifestyle change, we use money as a defense against change. "I'd probably have to take a cut in pay." Rationalization is sought through the tangible defense—money—rather than the intangible—fear of failure.

Our employers understand the "scorecard." They realize that money is chiefly a dissatisfier and that the purpose of pay, in reality, is to minimize frictions and cool off the passions that arise when pay dissatisfaction emerges. Employers accept this because their experience confirms it. If you pay people to keep them from becoming too unhappy rather than to inspire their efforts toward results, money becomes "a bromide for work upsets."

This is why our employers find it necessary to maintain equitability. They even follow one anothers' pay practices very closely so that the pay scales for comparable jobs are similar. This accounts for the standardization of pay we frequently encounter. Thus we find that the "scorecard" advantages that may be gained by changing employers (within the same occupational area) are marginal, and that is precisely what the employment system in our country is designed to accomplish!

Most salary increases and employee benefit plans do *not* provide an increment that is large enough to motivate any action other than the passive one of staying put—so we "postpone!" Remember, the serfdom of medieval Europe was originally an "employee benefit" eagerly sought by the peasants. It guaranteed to a weak person the protection of a powerful lord. It guaranteed to poor people the enjoyment of their meager holdings of land. It shielded against greedy tax officials. Yet within one generation, it turned into loss of freedom.

In contrast, we are in the serfdom of medieval Europe, an "era of aspirations." We are spending increasingly larger shares of our incomes for goods and services which reflect our lifestyle desires. The implications point to another kind of serfdom!

As Dr. George Katova, author of *The Mass Consumption Society*, elaborates: *"If what you have today appears insufficient tomorrow, disapointment and frustration may become frequent occurrences. Stress, tension and anxiety may even grow far beyond what has prevailed in less affluent societies. . . . The higher the aspirations, the more chance that people will be disappointed."*

Where do you belong? In the past twenty-five years, the distribution of income has made dramatic changes, altering social and economic lifestyles. The national-income statistics can be visualized in a diamond shape, with most of us in the middle, fewer at the bottom, still fewer at the top. What's your scorecard?

My $corecard

1. What level is your current income? Check the appropriate area. Are you comfortable with your current lifestyle? Position?
2. Where do your lifestyle aspirations rank? Check the appropriate area. What social implications do your aspirations have for you?
3. To what extent will you have to risk financial security to achieve life and career options? Explain.

_____

_____

_____

4. Compare your $corecard with that of a role model, mentor, or intimate.

	Current income	Lifestyle aspirations
Affluent: $75,000 and over (less than 1 percent of households)	_____	_____
Upper-Middle: $38,000–$75,000 (7 percent of households)	_____	_____
Middle: $22,500–$38,000 (25 percent of households)	_____	_____
Lower-Middle: $15,000–$22,500 (25 percent of households)	_____	_____
Below average: $7,500–$15,000 (25 percent of households)	_____	_____
Poor: $7,500 and below (17 percent of households)	_____	_____

Many people engage in life and career planning to seek new insights into designing their scorecards. Money is their primary obstacle in making changes. They say, "How can I make changes in my life with all these financial responsibilities? It's easy for *you* to make changes; you don't have kids! You have two incomes! You don't have a house! You've saved enough!" And so it goes—*the postponed life* continues.

How do you make the change? We always give the same advice: "You just do it!" Money will come when you're doing the right thing. Few believe what we say. Consider a few of the styles of coping that people have used to deal with the money issue, however:

- Figure out on paper exactly how much you are talking about. We operate on myths and fear in the money area.
- Adhere to a strict, barebones budget.
- Start saving now for the future goals you have.
- Share the risk with a partner; start slowly and small.
- Refinance your home or move to a smaller one.
- Creatively moonlight.
- Borrow money.
- Depend on spouse's income or make arrangements with a friend to take turns with expenses.
- Sell all your seldom-used possessions.
- Reduce your lifestyle temporarily; use your vacation money to further your goal.
- Form an inventure society to design new financial alternatives.
- Others: _____

What we must ask first is not how much money we need to prosper, but what conditions of life and personal relations are necessary to make us happy. What do you want the quality of your life to be? That's the optimum scorecard. Then what will it take financially to make that happen? We're often surprised at the answer!

Skills, the Root of All . . . .

 # 15

Many of us think of ourselves as roles, as titles. And then we determine our personal status and worth by the amount of prestige and recognition those titles suggest. Oftentimes, money is associated with the status, although not always. Imagine yourself at a party, overhearing these introductions:

"Hello, who are you?"

"I'm Sally. I'm Jim's wife. Jim is over there with Mr. Helm, the president of the company. What's your name? And what do you do?"

"Well, Sally, I'm Herb. I'm the treasurer of this operation. And this is my wife, June."

"Hello, June. Do you work too?"

"No, I'm just a housewife."

Despite all our new awarenesses, we still hear people saying these things. So far, we know nothing about Sally except that her spouse talks to the president. June has just put herself down, not because of what she does, but because of the way she portrays herself. Herb started the whole thing and now is at a dead end. Where would you go with the conversation now?

Our job titles seem to speak louder than "who we are." Role or title myths often rule the way we treat one another and ourselves. Several myths are most commonly used: paid employment is better than not; "women's work" is degrading; the more powerful the position, the more impressive the person; working with your hands is not as prestigious as working with your head;

the status of academic jobs outweighs the financial rewards; service occupations ought to expect low pay; business, though stressful, holds long-term financial rewards; there are many jobs women should never attempt; you can always fall back on sales.

Of course, *all* of these myths are being challenged now and rightly so, because we are learning that there is more to work than titles, prestige, and money. Besides, job titles tell us little, if anything, about what a person does during the day, what skills are used, and what special qualities that person brings to the job. Think of the difference among a homemaker who has a retarded child to care for, another who is a poetry writer, and another who is president of the League of Women Voters.

In this chapter, you will be introduced to an alternative way to think about your skills in relation to your work and daily activities—a way that will make sense and will stress what you can *do,* what you're *good at,* and what you *like* to do—rather than giving you a title that automatically categorizes you. Other people determine 75 percent of their opinion of you by the way in which *you* present yourself to them. The other 25 percent is determined by your actual work, skills, and reputation. If *you* are not aware and convinced of your skills, qualities, special traits, wants, and interests, you can't expect others to read your mind and know them. Not even your spouse or closest friend can do that.

A woman shared this story recently. "I've been to several consciousness-raising and support groups in the last few years. They really helped me to see that I was kind, sweet, real, nice, attractive, and important. But not until I looked at my skills in this life and career-renewal group did I know what I *can do,* what my marketable skills are, and how I'll fare in the work force in the future. I now know that I've got some real skills to reinforce my worth—and it's the thing I needed most."

A young man who was changing jobs and chose to take a three-month break between jobs had a lot of trouble with people asking him what he was doing. His sense of humor helped him considerably. He kiddingly chose several occupations that he thought would describe his activities. He was a private investor (he did have $50 worth of stock), or he was a money manager (he balanced his checkbook), or he was a free-lance artist (he painted his kitchen)!

THE SKILLS TREE

Skills are a constant part of our everyday vocabulary: "I'd like to go back to work, but I'm not sure I have the right skills." "To shift careers, I'd have to go back and be retrained." "I graduated with four years of college and no skills to get a job." However, few of us can even define the term "skill" (much less state what our own skills are).

One of the key parts of the excursion process is to focus on your skills—particularly those you would most enjoy using at this point in your life cycle. Identifying skills is a difficult task for most of us. A simple and concrete tree analogy will illustrate the three important skills areas that you possess (fig. 15.1).

1. *The root system:* Each tree must acquire food and water at least partially through its root system. The roots are not visible above the ground, but are necessary to the growth and development of the tree. The roots do most of the work to support the tree and seek out nutrients.

2. *The soil:* The soil is the medium in which the tree grows. The soil must contain nutrients that can be transmitted by the roots to the tree so that the growth of the tree can be maximized. If the soil is depleted of nutrients or lacks moisture, eventually the tree will show the effects.

3. *Species:* There is quite a difference between a palm tree and a flowering crab, an evergreen and an elm or maple. They are all separate species, but live in different places, grow in different ways, and have unique phases or cycles.

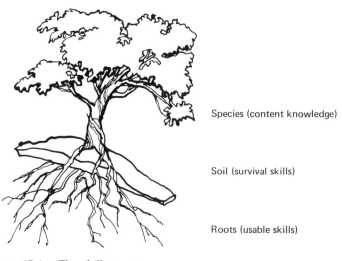

Species (content knowledge)

Soil (survival skills)

Roots (usable skills)

Figure 15.1.   The skills tree.

Root Skills

Just like our tree example, your root skills (root system) are not always ob-
viously visible, but they are your essential tools in performing in the world
of work. Your root skills are your portable, transferable, usable skills. They
are stated as actual things you can do (skills you have), and they express the
action you actually perform in work situations.

Root skills are the ones you take with you and use, no matter what job
you have, no matter where you are. You gain them from education, but
particularly from experience. So the more varied experiences you've had, the
more root skills you'll have. You carry your root skills with you, but may
have to use them occasionally to keep in practice. They are not the kind of
skills you leave in your desk when you complete a work activity or change
jobs. They are portable—they always go with you!

Here are some examples of root skills ("ing" indicates action):

learning	analyzing	filing
managing	singing	organizing
interviewing	designing	translating
lifting	directing	writing
listening	assembling	counseling
modeling	researching	

The intriguing thing about root skills is that we are always shocked at
how universal they are. The myth is that in different jobs or careers, there
are unique skills that only people in those career fields possess. This is usually
not the case. Counselors and salespeople, for example, use many of the same
root skills (listening, diagnosing, showing empathy). Similarly, both lawyers
and computer programmers use many of the same root skills (analyzing,
designing, strategizing, implementing plans). What is different for each are
the problems or content knowledge of their work.

Beyond a certain basic level of training in most fields, the way in which
you can best decide what you want to do next is to choose the root skills you
most enjoy using and look for jobs and careers that will enhance the use of
those skills. Often we let supervisors or random chance totally determine our
use of root skills on the job. We hope that our supervisor can read our minds
and magically choose the jobs that will make best use of our skills. Inventurers,
however, have seen the disappointments that mind reading brings. They are
willing to take the risk to share with their supervisors the root skills they have
and really enjoy using. Nine times out of ten, supervisors are thankful and
very relieved that they finally know enough information to make more constructive plans.

There is no simple test or way to find out what root skills you have,
although a number of ways have been attempted. The range includes me-

chanically scored tests, lengthy autobiographical papers, personal interviews, and previous work-assessment procedures. The best procedure for you will be partially determined by your learning style and by the amount of perseverance you have. So, prepare yourself for a skills workout on the Excursion-Skills Checklist that follows.

In addition to our Excursion-Skills Checklist, we also recommend John Crystal's autobiographical method and Dick Bolles's Quick Job Hunting Map as alternatives (see the bibliography). The Job Hunting Map and the Excursion-Skills Checklist are based on John Holland and Sidney Fine's categories of people and environments.

The Excursion-Skills Checklist

With the four excursion styles in mind, we have designed four different methods of approaching the checklist. Most of you have more than one style, however, and you may want to use more than one approach. Instructions for using the entire or long version are outlined in Appendix A.

1. *Option 1: Scan* the checklist in its entirety. Then go back to the beginning and in the column labeled *Overall impression,* put a check next to the skills that you generally feel you *can do* (because you have done them before). Now go back over those that you have checked and circle the skills you *enjoy* the most.

   Enter your circled skills on your excursion map (Box 14).

2. *Option 2:* Complete Option 1. In addition, complete the excursion-memo exercise in Appendix A, p. 168.

   Enter your most frequently used skill areas (artistic, consulting, persuading) on the excursion map (Box 14).

3. *Option 3:* Complete Options 1 and 2. In addition, complete the skills graph in Appendix A, p. 173.

   Enter your most used and enjoyed skills on the excursion map (Box 14).

4. *Option 4:* Complete Options 1, 2, and 3. Using the entire skills checklist, complete the quantity and quality section and find your total scores. Instructions are in Appendix A.

   Enter your scores on the excursion map (Box 14).

GROUP A—THINGS: REALISTIC

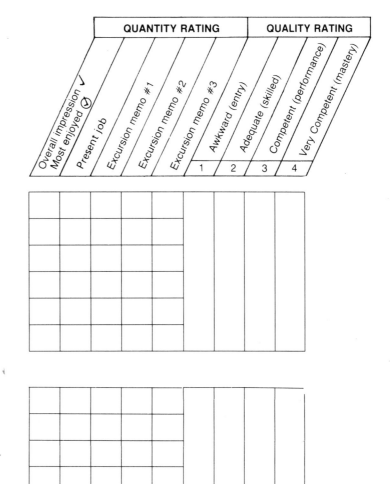

1. Physical Skills

   Using coordination and agility
   Outdoor—tennis, running, hiking,
     biking, camping, skiing, fishing
   Indoor—exercising, swimming,
     basketball, racketball, dancing

   Caring for plants, animals, farming

   Traveling, navigating skills

   Other:

2. Mechanical Skills

   Designing, shaping, composing
     objects and machines
   Setting up equipment, adjusting
     equipment, repairing, controlling
   Assembling, building with precision,
     operating
   Lifting, balancing, moving,
     selecting tools

   Washing, cleaning, tending
   Cooking, crafts (woodworks,
     needlework)

   Other:

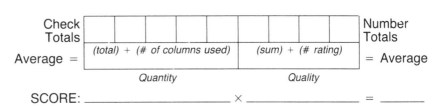

Figure 15.2.   Your excursion-skills checklist.

GROUP B—DATA: INVESTIGATIVE

1. Learning Skills

   Sensing, feeling, active involvement
   Observing, reflecting, perceptive of
     others
   Reasoning, abstract, using logic,
     data

   Experimenting, piloting, testing

   Estimating, assessing others

   Other:

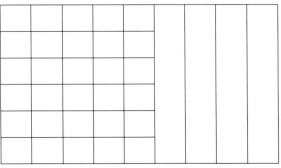

2. Decision-making Skills

   Clarifying problems
   Researching, surveying, analyzing,
     diagnosing problems

   Testing out ideas, troubleshooting
   Reviewing, critiquing, evaluating,
     choosing, inspecting (ideas)

   Other:

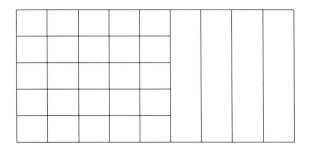

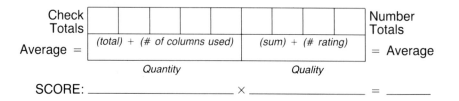

Check Totals / Number Totals

Average = (total) ÷ (# of columns used)   (sum) ÷ (# rating) = Average

Quantity   Quality

SCORE: _____ × _____ = _____

GROUP C—DATA: ARTISTIC

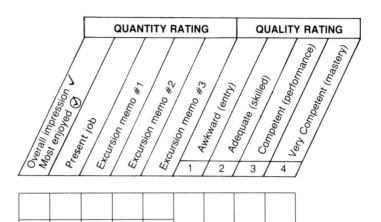

1. Creative Skills

   Imagining, intuiting, predicting
   Innovating, creating new ideas,
      experimenting
   Synthesizing, developing models,
      applying theory

   Perceiving shapes and design

   Other:

2. Artistic Skills

   Sensitivity to beauty

   Using facial expression, voice
   Symboling, visualizing, composing
      (music, poetry, photography)

   Designing visuals, fashions

   Directing productions

   Other:

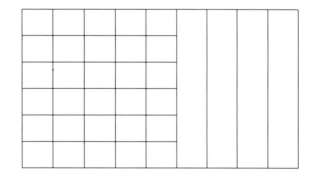

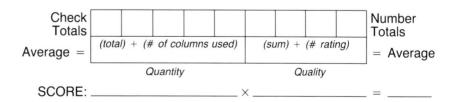

Check
Totals

Average = | (total) ÷ (# of columns used) | (sum) ÷ (# rating) |

Number
Totals
= Average

Quantity   Quality

SCORE: _____ × _____ = _____

GROUP D—PEOPLE: SOCIAL

		QUANTITY RATING				QUALITY RATING			
Overall impression / Most enjoyed	Present job	Excursion memo #1	Excursion memo #2	Excursion memo #3	Awkward (entry) 1	Adequate (skilled) 2	Competent (performance) 3	Very Competent (mastery) 4	

1. Communication Skills

   Speaking clearly, effectively

   Writing—reports, letters, memos
   Writing—promotional, creative,
      editing

   Reading—comprehension, speed

   Translating, explaining

   Other:

2. Instruction Skills

   Coaching, informing, leading,
      facilitating groups

   Designing educational materials
   Creating learning environments,
      events
   Illustrating theories and principles
      through examples

   Other:

3. Human Relations Skills
   Using counseling skills—empathy,
      rapport, patience, understanding
   Caring for, nursing, soothing
      others
   Managing office activities,
      atmosphere
   Negotiating, representing,
      advocating

   Other:

GROUP D—PEOPLE: SOCIAL (Continued)

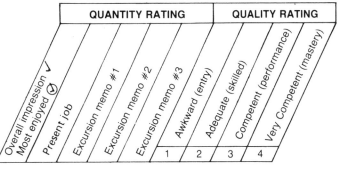

	QUANTITY RATING				QUALITY RATING			
Overall impression ✓ / Most enjoyed Ⓔ / Present job	Excursion memo #1	Excursion memo #2	Excursion memo #3	Awkward (entry) 1	Adequate (skilled) 2	Competent (performance) 3	Very Competent (mastery) 4

4. Mentoring Skills

   Listening and questioning others,
     reflecting, guiding, reviewing
   Diagnosing others, evaluating
     feelings, giving feedback
   Developing others, coaching, fore-
     casting, encouraging, motivating
   Sharing responsibility, problem
     solving, team building

   Other:

5. Consulting Skills (used in indirect
    reporting relationships only)

   Giving ideas, clarifying procedures,
     developing rapport
   Informing, advising, assisting,
     guiding, persuading others
   Conferring, diagnosing, discussing,
     resolving, cooperating
   Recommending alternatives, following
     through, evaluating

   Other:

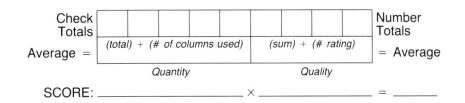

Check Totals / Number Totals

Average = $\dfrac{(total) + (\# \text{ of columns used})}{\text{Quantity}}$ | $\dfrac{(sum) + (\# \text{ rating})}{\text{Quality}}$ = Average

SCORE: _____ × _____ = _____

GROUP E—PEOPLE: ENTERPRISING

1. Leadership Skills

   Initiating activities, ideas

   Organizing time, self-direction
   Planning changes, anticipating
     problems

   Solving problems, using alternatives

   Risk taking, inspiring

   Other:

2. Managing/Supervising Skills
   Setting goals and standards,
     assigning tasks

   Organizing others, coordinating
   Planning, developing, organizing
     ideas
   Designing projects, procedures,
     timetables
   Evaluating progress, choosing
     alternatives, troubleshooting
   Implementing policies, responsi-
     bilities
   Evaluating performance of
     individuals

   Other:

GROUP E—PEOPLE: ENTERPRISING (Continued)

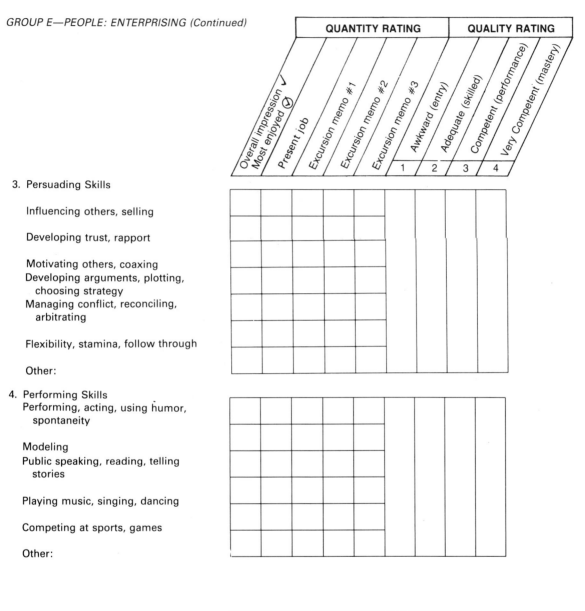

QUANTITY RATING

- Overall impression ✓
- Most enjoyed ⊘
- Present job
- Excursion memo #1
- Excursion memo #2
- Excursion memo #3

QUALITY RATING

- Awkward (entry) 1
- Adequate (skilled) 2
- Competent (performance) 3
- Very Competent (mastery) 4

3. Persuading Skills

   Influencing others, selling

   Developing trust, rapport

   Motivating others, coaxing
   Developing arguments, plotting,
     choosing strategy
   Managing conflict, reconciling,
     arbitrating

   Flexibility, stamina, follow through

   Other:

4. Performing Skills
   Performing, acting, using humor,
     spontaneity

   Modeling
   Public speaking, reading, telling
     stories

   Playing music, singing, dancing

   Competing at sports, games

   Other:

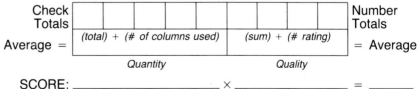

Check Totals   Number Totals

Average = (total) ÷ (# of columns used)   (sum) ÷ (# rating) = Average

Quantity   Quality

SCORE: _____ × _____ = _____

GROUP F—DATA: CONVENTIONAL

1. Detail Skills

   Keeping deadlines, details, accuracy

   Accepting responsibility, executing
   Making contacts, arrangements,
     brokering
   Organizing records, classifying,
     filing, processing

   Clerical skills, office machines

   Other:

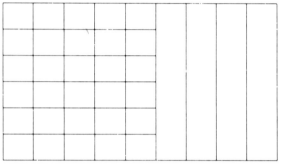

2. Numerical Skills

   Inventorying, classifying
   Using computational, statistical
     abilities
   Financial record keeping,
     appraising, projecting
   Managing budgets, money,
     allocating resources

   Other:

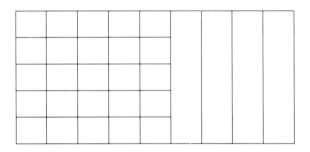

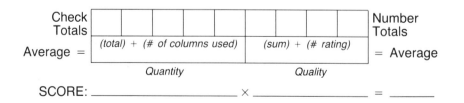

Check Totals

Number Totals

Average = | (total) + (# of columns used) | (sum) + (# rating) | = Average

Quantity   Quality

SCORE: _____ × _____ = _____

Survival
Skills

16

Survival skills are like the soil in which the tree grows (and flourishes). The soil needs to have the ingredients for growth, and the tree needs to be receptive to growth (climatized). For example, an evergreen tree in a tropical soil would not flourish, because the mix of elements is just not right for the tree and the weather conditions are not appropriate.

Your survival skills are composed of two parts: you as a unique human being with certain traits, moods, qualities, wants, and a personal style; and the environment around you, with its physical characteristics, rules, people, and distractions. Selecting an organization in which you can plant your root skills, and thus grow and flourish, requires a good definition, by you, of that proper soil. Survival on the job is linked to the best fit possible between you and your work environment.

Your survival skills are really your ability to read yourself and your environment. *These skills are so important that they are most often the prime factors in hiring, firing, demotion, and promotion.* You can spend months finding out which of your root skills are best and which you are really interested in using, only to be caught short by another set of factors—the mix of you and your environment. Many environments or organizations reward certain survival skills. You will be much happier in an environment that accommodates your best style.

Tom went sailing through the life and career-renewal experience, really pinning down lifestyle changes and root skills. He concluded that he definitely needed a job change and promptly started interviewing. He did a good job of sorting out which skills he wanted to use and impressed the interviewers. Well, he landed a good job in just a few weeks. But the first day of his new job, he decided that he was going to quit! What could possibly have happened? The people he was to work with, his coworkers, were really not his kind of people. These were things he'd never thought to ask about in the interview. A lesson well learned! (He didn't quit, but instead started thinking about his next job change and made some constructive changes in the present situation.)

People who have a good sense of their survival skills have the best chance of becoming inventurers—because they can choose more accurately the places in which they will and will not be happy. Many of us will take the first new option or job or individual or experience that comes along, just to ease the strain, fill time, or get out of limbo and feel better.

Your *single most important* survival information is your knowledge of your learning style. Review it on p. 33. This is the way in which you process and learn new information in your environment. You can work well with people of other learning styles if you can be somewhat versatile (use other styles) and appreciate the differences in styles. You will survive well if you capitalize on your most enjoyed style and blend it with the styles of others when you work as a team.

Your survival skills are really your ability to read yourself and your work climate. It takes wisdom to perceive the whole, to perceive essential relationships. The wise person is one who is able to "discern essential relationships" in a work environment to be able to make the best decisions possible, as early as possible.

> *We would like to train for wisdom not knowledge. And what we are training for is knowledge, because we can measure it. But knowledge is not convertible into human happiness and well-being. Wisdom is, because wisdom is learning how to live in harmony with the world.*
>
> Ram Dass

Learning Style and Survival

Take a moment to review your Learning Style highlights in chapter 5. Look at the strengths listed for your style, note the phrases that have meaning to you, then, consider the following questions:

1. What are the strengths of my learning style?

2. What implications do my style strengths have for choosing/surviving in a career environment?

3. How can I use my style more effectively in working with bosses, peers, clients, etc., whose styles differ from mine?

4. My level of flexibility—the ability to shift learning styles depending on the situation—rates as follows: (check one)

    _____ extremely flexible, sometimes wishy-washy
    _____ very flexible, generally shift to cope in diverse situations
    _____ patterned, change only if required by authority figure
    _____ rigid, unable to leave my comfort zone
    My closest friend/colleague tells me my level of flexibility is _____.

Another part of your survival package is your interpersonal communication skills. Here's your chance to be a little clearer about the communication qualities that contribute to your survival skills. Have some fun with this and share it with the members of your inventure network.

Interpersonal Communication Skills

1. *Step 1:* Complete this form quickly, without thinking too much about each item

2. *Step 2:* For each of the following items, circle the number that best describes the degree to which the statement fits you.

3. *Step 3:* Have someone else complete the scale the way he or she sees you.

4. *Step 4:* Compare your ratings with the other person.

1. Listening to others:	Low	1	2	3	4	5	High
2. Stating clearly what I mean:	Low	1	2	3	4	5	High
3. Understanding someone else's meaning:	Low	1	2	3	4	5	High
4. Tendency to interrupt:	Infrequently	1	2	3	4	5	Frequently

5. Initiating comments or suggestions:	Few	1 2 3 4 5	Many
6. Getting others to express ideas:	Infrequently	1 2 3 4 5	Frequently
7. Stating feelings to others:	Infrequently	1 2 3 4 5	Frequently
8. Awareness of others' feelings:	Low	1 2 3 4 5	High
9. Accepting feedback:	Low tolerance	1 2 3 4 5	High tolerance
10. Using tact:	Infrequently	1 2 3 4 5	Frequently
11. Trusting others:	Low trust	1 2 3 4 5	High trust
12. Tolerance of differences and others' opinions:	Low tolerance	1 2 3 4 5	High tolerance
13. Seeking close personal relationships:	Few	1 2 3 4 5	Many
14. Influencing others:	Few	1 2 3 4 5	Many
15. Reacting to affection:	Low tolerance	1 2 3 4 5	High tolerance
16. Reacting constructively to conflict:	Low tolerance	1 2 3 4 5	High tolerance
17. Level of self-awareness:	Low	1 2 3 4 5	High
18. Level of versatility:	Low	1 2 3 4 5	High
19. Seeking appropriate solutions:	Infrequently	1 2 3 4 5	Frequently
20. Monopolizing conversations:	Infrequently	1 2 3 4 5	Frequently

Key: Items 2, 3, 5, 7, 12, 14, 16, 18, and 19 focus on task or problem-solving skills.

Items 1, 6, 8, 9, 10, 11, 13, 15, and 17 focus on relationship or people-oriented skills.

Items 4 and 20 focus on blocking or nonfunctional skills.

What kind of an environment best suits your set of attributes and style? Remember, you can "have your act together," but still be in an environment that does not encourage your skills or suit your style.

Summarize your style and communication skills for the excursion map (Box 15).

The following questions focus on working-condition preferences, patterns of interaction, tolerances, and priorities. Answering these questions will help you not only survive in a work environment, but also succeed in job interviews. Personnel people tell us that successful candidates for jobs know what they want and what kind of an organization is the right place for them. Life and career renewers frequently tell us, "I want to work with people." That's about as descriptive as saying, "I want a job I will like." After all, morticians work with people too. Working through the following list of questions should help you arrive at more exact impressions of your preferred work environment.

Work Environment

What would ideal working conditions consist of for you? Sometimes it helps to think of the worst environment you've been in or can think of and note the elements present. Then think of the other extreme, or ideal conditions.

	Ideal*	Worst
Geographic areas	_____	_____
General area (suburb, city, rural, etc.)	_____	_____
Organization size (500 +, 50–100, 10 or less, alone)	_____	_____
Physical space (outdoors, indoors, privacy, open, office, plant)	_____	_____
Dress norms (business attire, casual, etc.)	_____	_____
Hours of work (9–5, flextime, part-time, etc.)	_____	_____

How have you tended in the past to adapt or react to environments you did not feel comfortable with? Check the behavior most appropriate to you:

  _____ Mold yourself to the situation

  _____ Expect the environment to change and silently complain

  _____ Negotiate for change on both parts

  _____ Leave

How much is environment a factor in your job satisfaction?

0% _____ 25% _____ 50% _____ 75% _____ 100%

*To complete this exercise you may prefer to follow the Visualization Sequence in chapter 9.

People Environment

The better the match between your people preferences and the work situation, the greater the chances for satisfaction and a productive relationship; the greater the mismatch, the greater the chances for dissatisfaction and a less-productive relationship. What kind of people environment are you best-suited for?

Work History

Reflect on your work history, concentrating on key jobs and their effect on you. Your work history can be used to discover how relationships with people have influenced your work satisfaction.

The *best* job I ever had was _____.

- The type of people I worked under were (bosses)

  _____.

- The kinds of people I worked with were (coworkers)

  _____.

- The kinds of people I served were (clients)

  _____.

The *worst* job I ever had was _____.

- The type of people I worked under were (bosses)

  _____.

- The kinds of people I worked with were (coworkers)

  _____.

- The kinds of people I served were (clients)

  _____.

Did any factors or pattern emerge, which will suggest the degree of fit

between you and career situations? Explain: _____

_____

_____

_____

What percentage of time would you prefer (25%, 75%, etc.):

    Working alone _____

    Working on a team _____

Do you prefer dealing with people (Yes or No):

    Individually _____

    Small groups _____ What size? _____

    Large groups _____ What size? _____

    As a leader _____

    As a manager/supervisor _____ Of how many? _____

    As an assistant _____

    As an equal _____

Compare your ideal work and people environments with the exercise "Why Do I Work?" on pp. 98–99.

    Enter your *most important* working conditions on your excursion map (Box 16).

What Species . . . ?

17

Now let's look at the tree from another perspective. The species of tree you are is the *subject matter*, or *special knowledge*, you have acquired, the field you're in, your college major, the product you sell, or service you render. The world has usually identified you according to your species and titled your work accordingly. Here are some examples:

Mental retardation (specialist)
Law, lawyer
Manufacturing (specialist)
Education, educator
Accounting, accountant
Automobiles (specialist)
Dentistry, dentist
Aging (specialist)
Humanities (specialist)
Foreign languages (specialist)
Wood products (specialist)

Chemical dependency (specialist)
Psychology, psychologist
Computers (specialist)
Insurance, insurance agent
Personnel, personnel officer
Plant biology, biologist
Preschool children
Architecture, architect
Radio/TV (specialist)
Marketing, marketer
Politics, politician

You can usually identify knowledge or subject matter because it has a language built around it. We call it jargon. Educators don't understand engineers; biologists don't speak "legalese." It is important to have content or subject knowledge, because that's where we put our root skills to work. We learn the subject matter in school or in advanced training and put that knowledge to work in a discipline or a field by using our root skills. When we leave that area or career, we shed our work-content focus, but carry with us our same root skills to our next job or career.

126

One of the most important elements in career/life planning is to decide the areas of interest or areas of special knowledge that you would be motivated to put your skills to work on! Unless you are interested in something you will see no way to put your skills to work.

Your Interests Pyramid

Interests are sometimes difficult to think about, so we are going to attack the subject from several angles. On the pyramid in fig. 17.1 are a number

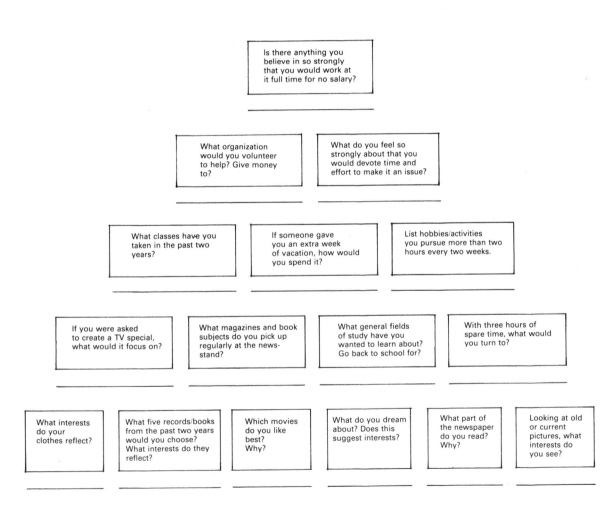

Figure 17.1. Your pyramid of interests.

of questions relating to interests. We use the pyramid to give you a chance to build your levels of interest on one another and figure out which are most important.

Step 1: Answer the bottom level first, then the second, third, fourth, and fifth. Write your answers under the boxes.

Step 2: Go over all the levels and check any interests that appear twice. Circle interests that occur more than twice.

After completing the exercise, answer the following questions:

1. Are most of your interests related to people _____ data _____ things _____?
2. Were you surprised at your repeated interests? Why? Why not?
3. Summarize the kinds of problems, issues, people, products, etc., you believe you might like to work with:

Enter your repeated key life interests on your excursion map (Box 17).

Special Knowledge and Experience

Step 1: In the column labeled Organization Areas of Interest, list the areas (e.g., departments, divisions, work units, subsidiaries or product areas) within the organizations that you have a knowledge of or expertise in at the three levels noted (elementary, more advanced, very advanced). For example, if you listed marketing, you would have at least a minimal *knowledge* of what the marketing function is, an understanding of what *knowledge* might be required in this function, and possess at least a rather elementary level of this knowledge.

Step 2: In the column labeled Knowledges I Picked Up in School or in Courses, list your classroom knowledges. Be sure to consider schools, colleges, conferences, workshops.

Step 3: In the column labeled Areas I Would Like to Learn More About, indicate any areas you have a strong interest in learning more about.

Enter your highest knowledge areas on your excursion map (Box 18).

THE DEGREE OF KNOWLEDGE I POSSESS (in my own estimation)	ORGANIZATIONAL AREAS OF KNOWLEDGE	KNOWLEDGES I PICKED UP IN SCHOOL OR IN COURSES	AREAS I WOULD LIKE TO LEARN MORE ABOUT
RATHER ELEMENTARY			
MORE ADVANCED			
VERY ADVANCED			

You Only Go Around Once

18

Suppose you could enclose all the information you have gathered to date and put it in the magic envelope, then send it to us and we would tell you the ideal lifestyle or job for you. If we could do that, we'd have solved the biggest career problem of all time.

First, there is no ideal job, since all jobs have some aspects that are part drudgery. Second, there is no magic way to take all of your abilities, skills, and interests and link them to *a* job. There are more than likely a number of career areas or jobs that might fit. But all is not lost. There are several exciting things you can do to get a better perspective or handle on your lifestyle and your career.

Everyone goes about the change process a little differently. You have your own learning style, your own way of taking risks, your sense of timing, and your own personal contacts. Past experiences predict that when you're ready, you'll "do it," but that readiness is an individual thing. For some, it means getting sick and tired of the present circumstances; for others it's making a change at the peak of success. Some people need friends to give them a swift kick; others change as a result of life events. Boredom moves some; too much activity convinces others. Everyone who's reported a change cites different "straws" that broke their backs or different reasons for change. Here's what some people have done on their way to becoming inventurers.

- A fifty-year-old educator had a shock realizing that he definitely did not want to retire, but would be forced to. His wife attended law school and was quite satisfied. Over dinner one night, they decided that he would get his law degree too and that they would begin practicing law together. He now attends law school at night and is well on his way to his second career.

- A twenty-eight-year-old college recruiter decided to call it quits with his job. He literally leaped at a chance to sell recreational products, because his interest was so high in the area and his skills included sales. He failed to realize that the amount of travel and socializing involved did not suit his personality. It took him another several months to locate a more desirable position within the recreation industry. Now he is much happier and more satisfied.

- A successful writer had advanced to editor of a magazine, only to find that she was competent but not totally interested in the administrative role. After much deliberation, she found a good and trusted colleague who agreed to share a job. They wrote a job-sharing proposal to her supervisor. It was so convincing that after a lengthy discussion, it was accepted as a pilot. It has been working successfully for several months, and now, in addition to her administrative duties, she can still write.

- An urban minister was determined to make a valid lifestyle switch—from being a workaholic to combining work with family leisure even during the week. He announced to his family one weekday evening that they were all going on a family bike ride to breakfast the next morning. It was a disaster. His spouse had other plans that she didn't want to break, and to the kids, biking during the day was "no big thing." But they went! One daughter almost got hit by a bus, and the restaurant wasn't open when they arrived. He learned a great lesson for himself. Changes take thinking and planning in advance, and those affected by the changes should be included in the decisions.

- A bank president going through a midcareer reassessment decided to make a lifestyle and job change. She wanted to live in a small town and be comfortable financially. She conducted personal research for nine months, talking to everyone she knew who could help her. She made the switch by buying a prosperous bank in a smaller town near a metropolitan area. She lives on a lake and rides her bike to work—and feels ten years younger.

- A sixty-five-year-old woman retired from her administrative job and decided to take advantage of her curiosity and love for learning. She enrolled at a local college (at senior citizen tuition rates) and started work toward her B.A. degree in literature. It'll take her eight years, but she loves every minute of it. She also walks two miles every day. Her friends think that she's getting younger, not older.

- A thirty-six-year-old homemaker who'd always dreamed of operating her own bookstore decided to get her feet wet, but not to drown. She got a part-time job in a local bookstore and is now learning all she can about the trade. She's asking questions, volunteering for things so she can learn each new aspect of the job, and paying careful attention to every detail. It's so much fun learning, she may increase her hours—and who knows, she may be manager some day.

- A psychiatric nurse who worked mostly with children decided after several years that he wasn't suited to the environment—the hospital, the emotional intensity, the hours, and the line of command. He decided to make an abrupt career switch, because otherwise he might never do it at all. He took a wild chance at real estate, which had been mentioned to him as an independent career (his primary work value!). He plunged right into it, took the ups and downs in stride, and organized his own counseling approach to selling homes. Now he's developed a program for prospective home sellers and buyers, based on his experience. He's never been so excited about work. He works nine months and then travels three.

- A corporate secretary wanted to further her career within the company. She asked her supervisor to send her to seminars and in-service training to increase her skills with people and management. Soon she was recognized for her initiative and skill and was assigned to a special project. She performed so well that she was slowly eased into a staff function in the education division. Along the way, she acquired a B.A. degree so that she would be ready for the next advancement. She's now a successful instructor and supervisor.

- A couple who were both pleased with their jobs decided to make some lifestyle changes; she was mostly responsible for the child-care and household duties. They realized it was because neither was experienced in the other's roles. She took classes to learn home-maintenance skills, and he learned to cook. After some initial awkward attempts at the new activities, they found they enjoyed the wide range of skill and activity. They also shared the child-care responsibility. He has even taken the child with him on some work trips to broaden his experiences with parenting.

- Two thirty-five-year-old attorneys dissatisfied with their law firms got to talking about their philosophies of work and life as a result of a life/career-planning course. There were some specific ways of operating that they both felt strongly about. They decided during the course to go into private practice together. After much lengthy discussion and lots of searching, they opened an office together. They both say it's the best thing they've ever done, even though it's still an experiment.

- A fifty-year-old male who was successful in his career but not sufficiently challenged got very interested in children with heart problems as a result of a grandchild's tragic illness. He devoted time and energy to publicity and campaigns and found numerous rewards in volunteer activity. He felt that he was being of service to others and to his own family, and this became one of his retirement goals.

- Two roommates decided that they greatly disliked their jobs and that they wanted to move to a city they both loved in another state. One of them could readily get a job there as an accountant, but the other would have more difficulty. They took a vacation there together to look around and make contacts. As luck (or fortuitous planning) would have it, a friend of a friend needed temporary help. They moved a month later, and both started working. Eventually, the temporary job collapsed, and one roommate had a period of unemployment. This time was used by agreement to get their house in order and to look for more meaningful work. A few months later, a professor friend quit his job, and it was exactly suited to the roommate. They now say it was one of the biggest and best risks they've taken.

- One forty-six-year-old man had become quite skilled in his computer-design job, but had become stale because of the sameness of his daily routine. He did a thorough self and work assessment and decided to propose a change to his manager. He proposed a team-project approach on the next work assignment, and after some negotiating, the manager decided to try the idea. It worked much better than expected, and now the man has other proposals in mind to keep his job interesting.

- A recent college graduate in advertising decided that his job was not totally satisfying, but that he wasn't ready to change. He decided to start a small operation on the side, through mail-order sales. He designed and produced hobby supplies for matchbook collectors (a need he saw around him) and is small but successful. He has met a challenge for himself personally—and this is just the first step!

- An attorney was practicing successfully, but not really living out her dream. For years, she'd studied and applied herself and was really getting weary. She decided to live out her dream before it was too late. She boarded a freighter in Los Angeles and is now proceeding around the world—her lifelong dream. She plans to return to the practice of law near a wilderness setting.

- One woman worked on the lifestyle exercises and realized that she wanted further counseling before she got involved in life or career exploration. After a few months, she felt ready to return to life/career planning, because she was more able to decide what she wanted for herself.
- A thirty-two-year-old educational program planner loved his job but was ready for a new challenge, something that would really test his skills and abilities. He decided to apply his skills to a long-term interest—music! He now gets paid to design unique musical experiences for corporations, conferences, reunions, department stores, shopping centers, and airlines.

These illustrations are designed to show you that the conclusion that you reach as a result of this chapter may be a very obvious one, or it could be earth-shattering at first. It may be that you'll make no change at all, a lifestyle change, an attitude change, a relationship change, a project change, a job change, a career change, or several of the above.

The end result we expect is *that you will know the excursion process (the steps) of life and career renewal in order to achieve balance and satisfaction in your own life.* If you know the process, you can go back and use it when you're ready. Growth occurs with change, and you can decide to create change. It is sometimes called a creative crisis. But life is too short to postpone. When will you decide to decide?

If you are ready and willing to put it all together and become an inventurer, then let's get on with it. There are several steps involved which you can do at your own speed.

Step 1:
Your Excursion Map

19

Go back and complete the boxes on your map that you left undone. Talk with other people to help you if necessary. You will not be able to generate new and exciting ideas unless you have gathered information about the most important subject of this excursion process—YOU.

STOP

Step 2: Inventuring

 20

First you might decide what action you want to take as a result of your inventuring:

1. Make lifestyle adjustments
2. Make major lifestyle changes
3. Start working or going to school
4. Stop working or going to school
5. Change work environment
6. Change work style and assignments
7. Change jobs within the same organization
8. Change job by moving to another organization
9. Change career

Here is an expanded list of specific options to get you thinking about your own. You will think of several other options, too.

1. Options within the work setting:
   a) Set new goals and standards
   b) Assess my attitude
   c) Tackle a new project
   d) Participate in in-service training
   e) Participate in reading program
   f) Pursue additional education

g) Change the emphasis of responsibility

h) Propose "on-loan" assignment to another part of the organization

i) Rearrange my work environment

j) Seek trial work on a different project

k) Join team project or task force

l) Make a recommendation or proposal

m) Consult with another department or division

n) Arrange to work with people you enjoy the most

2. Options outside the work setting:

 a) Creative moonlighting—second job

 b) Part-time employment—present or new job

 c) Capitalize on a hobby, physical activities

 d) Volunteer activities, community, professional—get active in clubs, organizations, church, politics

 e) College classes or degree (present or new subject area)

3. Options for career or lifestyle change:

 a) Partial career switch—your current skills in a new area

 b) Total career switch—new skills, new area of work

 c) **Stop to rethink—travel, relax, do nothing, unemployment**

 d) Sabbatical

 e) Move to a new geographical location

 f) Leave of absence

 g) Retire—on time or early or not at all

 h) Dual career—share a job with someone

 i) Spouse work—or switch roles

Now you need a little help from your friends. You want as many ideas as you can possibly get from people as to what you can do, given your excursion-map information. You'll need good brainstormers, because you want lots of options, even if you only end up choosing a couple.

Even if you want to make a small environmental change, it's worthwhile completing this exercise. You can get much more specific suggestions after you get the broader ones. If you're making lifestyle or job changes within organizations, you'll want to gear the brainstorming more specifically after you get the broad perspective. Do this individually or in a small group, but *be sure to do it*. Form an inventure society or a personal board of directors for assistance on your excursions. It is vital that you get several creative options both in lifestyles and careers so you can start the next step in the process.

Encourage people to dream and to be farfetched, to get outside the ruts of usual thinking. You can test reality later.

1. Begin by giving people the following exercise. (Do it yourself first.) This will test their readiness to explore options with you.

Connect These Nine Dots with Four Straight Lines

1. Do not lift your pencil once you start.

2. Do not go back over lines; you can cross lines.

See answer in Appendix B.

2. You'll find that it's easier to think of options by looking at specific pieces of information. You'll do it by forming a simple equation (see examples on p. 139). Root skills are the key to the equation; without them, you'll have no grounding. Then you'll want to *apply* your root skills to something—on-the-job *interests*, *leisure* pursuits, or other *subjects, issues, life goals, basic life codes, fantasies*. Pick the areas you felt strongest about or that were easiest for you to complete.

3. Have your inventure network look at the different blocks on your excursion map and think of activities, lifestyles, and careers, using new combinations of your skills and interest. There are several ways to approach this; each varies with the kind of information you've collected and your style.

4. Have your network partner call out as many options as possible—they can be silly, farfetched, or seemingly unrealistic. You're not going to be held to any of the ideas. But you need a starting point. It is *imperative* that you have enthusiastic, interested people do this, or you could get bogged down here. Get at least ten ideas.

When people give you ideas to put into the hopper, listen and *write them down*, but *do not* start telling them why you can't do it, or don't want to, or why someone else won't let you. Practice open-mindedness and free expression. We'll get to realities next. It'll lead to lots of possibilities.

Here are a few brainstorming ideas that other groups have developed for one another. They were told to really dream! For out of dreams emerge ideas and motivation!

INVENTURE EQUATION

Root skills 1. 2. 3.	×	Interests, issues, life goal, on-the-job interest, fantasies, subject, or basic life values	=	Options
Consulting and traveling	×	Sports/ independence	=	Consultant with recreational ski areas. Farfetched? Not so! He's doing it!
Writing, mechanical, creating	×	Anthropology/ reading/ photography	=	Photo essays for magazines; edit anthropology-related publication. She's learning!
Researching, physical	×	Wilderness camping/ flying plane	=	Research director for camping-equipment company; fly out and test camping gear.
Administrating, managing	×	People/ travel/ French	=	Administrator of travel-incentive organization; sets up trips around world; goes to countries, free!
Mentoring, creating	×	Youth crisis/ crafts	=	Counseling youth in drop-in center (volunteer basis); works with arts/crafts.
Writing, public speaking, research	×	Arts/ foods/ religion as life goal	=	Started church orchestra and theater, then worked with church to write and publish guide to citywide church-related cultural events.

If you want to be more systematic in your brainstorming, use the following formula and come up with at least ten options for your life, your present work, or future work. The box numbers relate to the boxes on the Excursion Map. This example is from a nursing manager in a metropolitan hospital who wanted to renew her career.

Root skills +	*Interests* +	*Special Knowledge* +	*Life/Work Values* +	*Lifestyle Goals* +	*Life Purpose* +	*Fantasy* =	Options
Box 14	Box 17	Box 18	Box 19	Box 12	Box 11	Box 1	
managing	holistic	nursing-	expertness	balance in	outpatient	retreat	
persuading	health	oncology	variety	life/work	clinic for	center	
leadership	mushroom	psychology	service	develop	holistic	holistic ed-	
communi-	hunting			manage-	health	ucation	
cating	hiking			ment skills			
	fitness			education in			
				wellness			

Options (on-the-job plus future):

find a mentor in management to learn skills

take wellness courses

get involved in "visions" program in the hospital

independent study in nonprofit organization management

get involved in P.R. area of hospital

work one night a week in holistic clinic

manage hospice

camp nursing

go to retreat center on summer vacation

get into new development area of hospital or into outpatient area

join a professional organization of nurses interested in holistic health

attend wellness conferences

corporate nurse—wellness emphasis

set up fitness program for hospital personnel

Now It's Your Turn:

Root skills +	*Interests Issues* +	*Special Knowledge* +	*Life/Work Values* +	*Lifestyle Goals* +	*Life Purpose* +	*Fantasy* =	Options

Brainstorm:

The trick is to make sure that your best and most enjoyed skills were selected and that your most valued interest, issues, and subjects were explored. The broader your experience has been, the more opportunities you'll have to choose from. So, volunteer, take extra assignments, go to classes—expand your horizons. Sometimes you can use exactly the same skills—writing, designing, managing, teaching—but apply them to an area you are more interested in, such as social service, plants, recreational products, travel, philosophy. Or you can use your exact job skills and transfer them to another project within the job or organization. If you are interested in expanding your skills on your present job and want to approach your supervisor, dean, manager, or project director about it, use this career-growth proposal. It is a very useful tool for constructive negotiation and has worked for many. Be sure to do your homework before you use the proposal. The options are endless. The rest depends on you.

There are several other resources in addition to you, your friends, and mentors that you can use to assist you in putting it all together.

- Other workbooks and interest inventories—see the bibliography
- Reference material, e.g., *Dictionary of Occupational Titles, Occupational Outlook Handbooks*
- Some professional career counselors (but be careful!)
- Action-oriented course or support group
- Internships and related experiences

None of these is a substitute for doing this work on your own with your inventure network, but rather provides additional information that reinforces your decisions.

Some changes will be small, others large. You may find that what you want to do will take more time than you thought. Well, change always takes more time than we think it will. Expect any substantial change to take a year. That seems like a long time; but remember, you'll be working on the change the whole time. As time goes on, your first ideas will change somewhat, and the opportunities that arise may alter your goals a little. You are experiencing what are called tradeoffs. You get part of what you want, but give in somewhere else (sort of like buying a house or car!). What you must keep in mind are the things or qualities or ingredients you want most and what you're willing to do to obtain or ensure them. It all evolves once your mind is focused. Also, starting with small changes leads inevitably to bigger ones. It's catching! Don't be surprised when your friends get the bug too! Also expect ups and downs. The important thing is not that you have them, but how you handle them. More on this in Step 3.

CAREER-GROWTH PROPOSAL—I
(Present Position)

Name _____ Date _____

Job Title _____ Div/Dept. _____

Current objectives: In your own words list the important objectives or responsibilities for your job during the coming year.

_____

_____

_____

_____

_____

_____

_____

_____

_____

Skills required: Review the root-skills checklist and survival-skills exercises. List the skills *required* to complete your current objectives. Circle those skills for which you feel you need further know-how to satisfactorily perform your job. Add other factors (personality, climate, knowledge) you feel are important to your job.

_____   _____   Comments:

_____   _____

_____   _____

_____   _____

_____   _____

_____   _____

_____   _____

Proposal: To increase my effectiveness and satisfaction in my current position, the following things must occur:

	Action steps	*Target dates*
1.	_____	_____
2.	_____	_____
3.	_____	_____
4.	_____	_____
5.	_____	_____

Obstacles: What might get in the way?

_____

_____

_____

Reward: How will I reward my efforts?

_____

_____

_____

_____

Penalty: What if I don't finish my proposal?

_____

_____

_____

_____

_____

_____   _____

Completion date   My signature

                               _____

                               My supervisor's signature

CAREER-GROWTH PROPOSAL—II
(Future Position)

Name _____ Date _____

Proposed direction (or job area) _____

_____

_____

_____

Skills required: List the skills required in the new position area: (root, work content, survival)

_____   _____   Comments:

_____   _____

_____   _____

_____   _____

_____   _____

_____   _____

Your objective: Compare these skills with your own from your excursion map.

Position objectives: In your own words, list the important objectives or responsibilities in the new position.

_____

_____

_____

_____

_____

Proposal: Highlight the specific purpose of the new position and how your skills and abilities will apply to the particular problems or opportunities (use skills, past accomplishments and specific illustrations).

_____

_____

_____

_____

Benefits: Project potential benefits to the organization from selecting you for this position.

_____

_____

Salary: State the salary you expect in the new position.

_____

Active position search: List the steps required to move to the new position.

Action steps	Target dates
1. _____	_____
2. _____	_____
3. _____	_____
4. _____	_____
5. _____	_____

_____   _____
Completion date   My signature

Step 3: What Holds You Back

21

By this time you have more ideas than you know what to do with. You look around you at other people who've made changes, and it looks so easy, but now that it's staring you in the face, it never looked so hard.

Here's the spot where a lot of people get stuck. All the subtle reasons for not doing things or making changes creep in and now take on immense proportions. It's inevitable! We're creatures of habit and status quo. It's hard to change. It leaves us off balance temporarily. We're not sure of the results. We've never done it before. Limbo doesn't look so bad any more. There are other people involved. There are two major questions you can ask yourself to get a better perspective about this time:

1. *If not now, then when will I do it?*
2. *What's the worst thing that can possibly happen?* (Many people say, "I could still be doing what I'm doing now!!")

Don't run away from or hide your fears and resistance. Hit them head on and decide how you plan to cope with them. Here's an example to get you started.

Coping with Change

On the next page, circle on the left all the factors that assist you in making changes (or a specific change); on the right, circle your favorite reasons for not making changes.

For (promote) change
skills, motivation, a course, family support, self-confidence, someone's death, age, health, interests, experience, risk ability, fulfillment, praise (encouragement), purpose, friends, energy, time, a mission, ideas, education, a "shock," a role model, need for variety, a good offer, dissatisfaction, spouse, divorce, life stage, support-group pressure, new challenge, opportunity, geographical move

Against (deter) change
lack of skill, no motivation or course, family responsibility, high expectations, no confidence, lack of money, security, seniority, comfort, too old/young, illness, no interest, lack of experience, no focus, too safe, no contacts, low energy, no time, lack of education, fear of failure, fear or success, fear of unknown, commitment, low self-esteem, confusion

You have no doubt noticed the similarity in the two lists. You see, you can use anything as an excuse if you want to.

Enter your most important promoters and deterrents in the space provided next to the excursion map.

List ways to overcome or modify or challenge items in the right column by compromise, negotiation, creative alternatives, using resources in the left-hand column.

Look over the case studies in chapter 18 and talk to your inventure network about their suggestions. If you really want to do something, there's always some way.

Most people use money as the biggest block. If you do, reread the chapters on money and sincerely put yourself to the test. Perhaps it would be more fair to give yourself some time and a plan for working out finances rather than shelving an idea because you can't afford it. Family responsibility is another big reason for stagnation. But when you discuss change with your family, often they are very supportive after initial fears are voiced. You see, they'd rather live with someone who's doing more of what he or she wants to do and who is happy. You're not doing anyone a favor by "postponing" your life away for their sake. Test it out before you give up.

There are some additional factors to consider in making changes, based on your preferred learning style. Each learning style has different problems or traits that hold users back from making changes. Each style also has specific strengths that will help users to approach change in a most constructive manner. And that's how serendipity occurs. Serendipity is not magic, but rather a set of fortuitous events that happen when you are investigating what you really want to do and using your most comfortable style doing it! The following chart suggests some assets and liabilities users of each style will probably encounter.

Learning Styles and Change

	What Will Hold You Up?		What Will Help You?
Enthusiastic	No organization or goal setting; impulsive; so involved, they become splintered; loose ends are not always taken care of; becomes unbelievable to other people; changes jobs too quickly	Enthusiastic	Gets others involved; operates on intuition, "gut" reactions; takes risks with new experiences; very active when motivated; will talk to other people and get inspiration in process; may try several options
Imaginative	Afraid to change relationships; creates conflict or hurts people, so stays same; no change results with all the efforts, just good ideas; security with status quo; won't be pushed; waits too long for inspiration	Imaginative	Will generate lots of options for change; observes how others have made the change; uses creative hunches, plays with ideas; fantasizes, can see images; lets ideas integrate or come together before changing; can wait for the best timing
Logical	Needs too much evidence before acting; too cautious, slow, methodological; doesn't get involved with people; too bogged down in theory; wants too many guarantees; takes risks very slowly	Logical	Gathers relevant facts, logical order; very organized, feels more secure in change; reads books, looks at several approaches, double checks; uses resources well— libraries, information-search programs; analyzes

What Will Hold You Up?		What Will Help You?	
			options, calculates probabilities; can map out on paper before jumping in; works well alone
Practical	Doesn't use caution in action; task overrides people; hard to wait for anything; impatient; needs to control and do it alone; doesn't listen enough to others	Practical	Sees change as problem to be solved; uses detective skills to get facts; evaluates options, sets up trial situations; sets goals and acts, not bogged down; works well independently

One other thing to keep in mind is that your most comfortable style can leave you just that—most comfortable. There comes a time when logicals have gathered enough information, analyzed most of the options and must finally do something, act on it. Enthusiastic learners need to stop and figure out which of the many experiences they've had is worth pursuing further. Imaginers must take initiative to test out some ideas. And practical learners need to sit back and reflect on their experiments to see a broader view of the activity. Each of us has more than one learning style that we can use, and this is the time they are most useful. And the more flexible you can be, the more you can capitalize on your styles.

The actual point of change, the turning point, is achieved only after collecting all of the resources and weighting the uncertainties. Coping with uncertainty is called "risk taking." The goal of an inventurer is to turn risks into adventures. Some people can stand financial uncertainty far more easily than relationship uncertainty. Some people take physical risks more easily than risks with ideas. By using your main learning style to approach uncertainty (e.g., practicals seeing finances as a task or problem to be tackled on their way to a goal), once you get to the point of actually doing it or mulling it over afterward, it ceases to be such a risk. Logicals would probably analyze all options before plunging in; enthusiasts would most likely jump in and look later; practicals would tackle it only if it looked inviting; imaginatives would observe how others have done it and pick the best way in time.

You probably learned how to cope with uncertainty in your family, and you are better with some risks than with others. You've already rated your risk taking in the survival skills section. Now try to imagine how your own family would respond in the situations listed on the next page.

Coping Style

Financial
Loss of job or financial risk

_____

Major purchases

_____

Emotional
Big disagreement between two family members

_____

Divorce or separation

_____

Love or affection

_____

Intellectual
Sharing original ideas

_____

Differing with others' opinions

_____

Reading and discussing philosophy, science, poetry

_____

Physical
Trying new sports challenges

_____

Coping when in physical danger—storms, car accidents

_____

Family style of coping
What would parents do?

_____

_____

1. Do you follow these same patterns? How?

_____

_____

2. What kind of uncertainties are you best at coping with?

_____

_____

3. How can you consciously use your learning style to cope more confidently?

_____

_____

Enter your best coping style (financial, physical, emotional, intelligence) in the space provided next to the excursion map.

Step 4:
Reality Testing

22

With this step in the excursion process, you are beginning to reality test your self-assessment with life and career options in the real world. You've decided to work for a definite change. Perhaps your initial efforts in this process, depending on your learning style, were primarily introspective. All new data are evaluated in terms of compatibility with what you know about yourself. But now is the time to activate options or paths that you may wish to explore. Most of us have many options to choose from. You must identify "where" and "how" you can best utilize the unique dimensions of *you* that make up your excursion map.

None of us begins this active exploration process with a clean slate. We have had significant role models, mentors, and intimates who have influenced our views of various career paths. To pursue new directions without our own input of facts and reality testing could easily lead to a future of frustration. Reading all the literature and seeking advice from professionals in a number of fields still probably won't produce an absolute certainty about direction. The most useful reality testing is direct contact or experience. There is no substitute!

Several years ago we saw an Australian film called *Walkabout*. This provocative film is about a young Australian aborigine on his walkabout—a six-month solo excursion test in the wilderness, a rite of passage that precedes his acceptance into adult society. The movie was provoking in that it presented an analogy, or blueprint, for a challenging and appropriate process of reality testing.

The young native in the movie had to *demonstrate* that he had acquired the awareness and skills necessary to make him a contributor and a survivor in his society. By contrast, we are often faced with only safe paper-and-pencil experiences that test our awareness and skills, and often they are far removed from the actual experiences we will have in real life. Many times we do not allow ourselves to apply what we know in strange but real situations. And yet is it not clear that what really matters is not so much what we know about, but what we feel, what we stand for, and what we can do and will do?

In our opinion the "walkabout" is a useful analogy to guide us in exploring our own life and career options. The walkabout analogy suggests that your "reality testing" measure up to a number of criteria:

1. *Experiential*—your reality tests should be real rather than simulated; we must get out and experience—taste, touch, feel, smell, hear—the options we are exploring. One experience of breaking through the confines of your perceived limitations, one telephone call, one risk, are the seeds for further growth and are worth your full attention.

2. *Challenging*—your excursions should challenge and excite your capacities as fully as possible—urging you to consider every obstacle you put in your own way as a barrier to be broken through. Reality tests are challenges to your daring and skill in an unfamiliar environment—challenges to explore and to express your own imagination in some exciting form.

3. *Self-directed*—your excursions should be challenges you choose for yourself. The major challenge is in making decisions. In primitive society there are few choices; in ours there is a confusing array of options in lifestyle and work. Happiness depends on your ability to make appropriate choices for yourself. The competition is with yourself, not with others. The satisfaction is in the recognition by others of what you have proved to yourself—"This is what I can and will do!"

It is through "walkabout" experiences that we are able to choose options to work for. Fantasy becomes reality. We learn to trust our own experiences, judgments, and information and to rely less and less on what we perceive to be the judgment of society.

Society often fears the inventurer—people like you, exploring options that follow the dictates of your own conscience. Reality testing will make some people around you uneasy—spouses, friends, parents, employers, etc. The uneasiness or conflicts are the result of the fear we have of facing ourselves.

What kind of "triggering event" will have the power to focus your energy into action? What would be an appropriate and challenging "walkabout" for you?

Using a variety of resources will increase your knowledge of options and provide the reality testing needed to translate your interests into action. The first step is organizing yourself.

First of all, to reality test your ideas, it's necessary to scrap a number of well-entrenched convictions. This, you'll quickly discover, is easier said than done, for you'll only half believe, initially, the strategies in this chapter. You'll find yourself raising all sorts of objections, which is another way of saying that long-held beliefs and values are being threatened. Try not to make judgments, however!

Let's look at reality testing in terms of the active job search. Some of you are probably mumbling under your breath, *"It's a waste of time to organize an active job search. Everyone knows jobs depend on who you know and on luck (being in the right place at the right time)."* No one can argue with that! There are a number of factors influencing a successful answer that you can control. Why not maximize your luck by focusing your energy on those factors?

THE FOCUS PROCESS

The active career-hunting systems in our society are, at best, haphazard and castabout processes. In spite of the fact that all of us are involved in the job hunt at some time in our lives, very few of us really know how to go about it in a way that works to our maximum benefit. Ninety percent of the population goes about the job hunt in a random, disjointed manner. Perhaps it's because people don't know what they're looking for to begin with. Or perhaps it's because they don't know how. The focus process is a series of strategies to assist you in planning a systematic job search. It is based on the following strategies:

1. The key ingredient to the search is complete information and experience gathering. There is no substitute!

2. Employers hire solutions to problems. Jobs are really problems that need solving.

3. Employers offer jobs based on *abilities* that *you* communicate to them to solve their problems. Thus after the vital information gathering, 70 percent of the search depends on "becoming a candidate" and effectively presenting yourself as a solution to the problem.

The steps to implement these strategies are:
F Functional brief
O Occupational research
C Creative exploration
U Unique interviewing
S Supportive follow-up

Let's look at each step.

The Functional Brief

A functional brief is one of your major tools in the active job search. Your brief translates your excursion map into a format that makes sense to a potential employer. Often called a "resume," your brief states your case for you. It differs from a classic resume in several respects. First, it is functional. It is based on what you can offer and how you can solve the problem of a potential employer. It is *not* a laundry list of everything you've ever done, in chronological order. Second, it is brief. Like a lawyer's brief, it makes a highly persuasive case for you in about one minute or less—which is the average reading time allotted to this sort of tool.

Employers are busy people who often spend many hours reading the resumes of aspiring employees. There are probably as many opinions concerning the "perfect brief" as there are employment specialists. The bibliography contains books which will teach you, very capably, to develop your own resume or brief. Job-hunting experts such as John Crystal, Dick Bolles, Dick Lathrop, Bernard Haldane, and Howard Figler have developed excellent approaches to this subject. In conjunction with the assistance they offer, the following strategies may also help:

1. Create your own unique formula for a brief; don't follow any formula blindly.

2. Develop one now and keep it on hand; it tends to bolster your self-esteem even if you don't really need a job right now. Besides, writing it when you're feeling best about yourself will result in a better brief.

3. Consider these sections in your brief:

   a) *Objective:* the level and function (not job title) you seek. Focus on the likely needs of the employer.

   b) *Qualified by:* support your objective by showing "how" the scope and effect of your past experience can help solve the employer's problem. Use action verbs, e.g., managed, directed, sparked, accomplished, developed, saved.

   c) *Education:* education recedes in importance as an employment factor over time. Treat this section accordingly.

   d) *Other:* personal traits, interests, civic activities, honors, licenses, publications, professional memberships, etc. Focus on the needs of the potential employer.

Keep in mind that the primary purpose of your functional brief is to get you in front of a live person for an information-gathering or job interview.

Occupational Research

Armed with a functional brief which focuses on your objective and your best attributes, you should then gather information on the *occupational fields* that meet your objective, the *organizations* within those fields, and the *individuals* within those organizations. We mentioned earlier that the key is complete information gathering and experience. Stay in the information-gathering phase. The minute you say that you are seeking a job—slam!—you see doors shut. If you ask for information, however, people will open doors for you. We all like to share information with "allies"—people who are interested in the same subjects we are, or better yet even interested in us.

Sound difficult? Not really. Try it. Go back and briefly review chapter 5. Occupational research is accomplished best in your own unique learning style. Consider these options:

- Call or visit people in your "inventure network." Ask for information, but be sure you don't ask for jobs.

- Scan the yellow pages of your phone directory to get an overview of a field of interest. Visit or tour several of the organizations that seem most interesting.

- Visit your local library. Libraries are excellent resources for occupational research. The library is jammed with relevant occupational reading on all three levels—occupational fields, organizations, and yes, even individuals (*Who's Who in Business,* etc.).

- Set up an "inventure search team" of a personnel professional, librarian, employment agent, and mentor. Map a step-by-step information-gathering plan and checkpoints for completion.

The purpose of occupational research is to narrow your focus down to a manageable handful that truly turn you on. At the same time, you're trying to get a glimpse of the problems that those occupations, organizations, and subsequently interviewers are most concerned with. The next step is then to explore those in more depth.

Creative Exploration

You've finally settled on several organizations that really interest you. Now, how do you get in to see the person(s) in the position to hire you? This step calls for all the courage and energy you can muster!

Numerous surveys have been conducted by the Department of Labor as well as private organizations to determine the most effective methods of making the "job connection." Typically the studies show that out of an average cross section of one hundred people, here is how the "job connection" was made:

1% private agency	6% school placement	48% inventure network
3% public agency	24% direct contact	13% combination
5% want-ads		of the other six

We don't like those data any more than you probably do. But experience backs those figures up very solidly. Common sense would indicate that you should spend roughly three-quarters of your active job-search efforts on the informal exploration system—contacting people and places directly and seeking assistance from your network. Dick Bolles's excellent book, *What Color Is Your Parachute?* discusses this in more depth.

Unique Interviewing

There is quite a difference between interviewing for information and interviewing for jobs. The former is designed to explore work areas, interests, people, skills, climate, and values of various jobs or organizations. The job interview focuses on a specific job with the intent of becoming the best candidate if the match is right for you. Interviewing for information should be done prior to job interviewing. Let's look next at job interviewing.

All of your efforts up to this point have been designed to open the door to a job interview. You must now rely on your performance in the interview to secure the position.

The interview is an opportunity to match your skills and interests with *one* way of using them. In addition to convincing the employer that you are the best candidate to solve the problem, the interview should also help you determine if this is the best career path for you—a 50–50 situation.

Consider the interview in two phases: (1) phase 1—preparing for the interview, and (2) phase 2—the interview. Let's look at these phases separately.

Phase I—Preparing for the interview
It is only through planning and anticipating your interview performance that you can present yourself in the most focused manner. The ingredients here are the same as those mentioned earlier.

Preparing for Your Interview

1. *Step 1:* Find a comfortable position and talk yourself through the relaxation exercise (see pp. 69–70).

2. *Step 2:* Think about a potential or upcoming interview. Envision a mental picture of yourself in that interview.

   a) What is your image of yourself?

   b) What image do you think the interviewer has?

   c) How is the way you talk, walk, dress, act, and *listen* likely to affect the interviewer?

   d) What type of image do you project in relation to your chosen area of work?

3. *Step 3:* Develop answers to each of these questions out loud in a "dry run."

   a) Why should I hire you?

   b) Why are you leaving your present situation?

   c) What two or three accomplishments have given you the most satisfaction? Why?

   d) In what kind of work environment are you most comfortable?

   e) What do you know about our organization?

   f) What major problem have you encountered and how did you deal with it?

   g) What criteria are you using to evaluate the organization for which you hope to work?

   h) What specific personal goals have you established for yourself in the next five years?

   i) How long would you stay with us?

   j) What pay do you have in mind?

   k) What would you do to improve our operations?

   l) What kind of relationship should exist between a supervisor and subordinate?

   m) Tell me about yourself.

   In preparing for the interview, use the following checklist:

Have I
Yes   No

Yes	No	
_____	_____	Learned about the organization?
_____	_____	Learned about the work/job/problem?
_____	_____	Learned about the interviewer?
_____	_____	Decided which problems my skills can help solve?
_____	_____	Listed my questions?
_____	_____	Prepared a functional brief (to send before or leave after the interview)?
_____	_____	Listed my references?
_____	_____	Confirmed the appointment and time frame?
_____	_____	Scouted the "survival" environment?
_____	_____	Thought of my purpose going in?
_____	_____	Thought of my plan of action coming out?

At some point in the interview, the employer will ask if you have any questions. If not, be sure to take the initiative, early on, to ask yours. Specific questions you might consider listing ahead of time are the following:

1. Would it be all right if I asked you a few questions?
2. Would you mind describing the duties of the job for me?
3. What abilities do you need most (least?) in people on this job?
4. What is the largest single problem facing you now? Is there a specific problem with (quality work, increased production, greater efficiency, lower waste in time, effort, and/or materials)?
5. Could you tell me about the people I would be working with?
6. What are the primary results you would like to see me produce?
7. Do any factors prevent action along this line?
8. Have you had a chance to review my functional brief?
9. Did it raise any questions about my qualifications I can answer?
10. May I check back with you on (specify when)?

Phase II—The interview
Interviewing styles vary considerably, but most involve a fairly even give and take. Flexibility is the key. You can relax and let things flow if you have prepared carefully before the interview. By doing your homework, interviewing can actually be fun.

Several interview strategies might be useful:

1. What learning style do you think the interviewer is? What type of information is that style most comfortable with?

Will like success stories, actual experiences, enthusiasm, inspiration.

Will be interested in the way you relate to them, how interesting you are, how friendly you are.

Will be interested in facts, prior experience, details about your skills, abilities.

Will be interested in problems you've solved, accomplishments, results, new ideas you have.

2. Be alert to nonverbal clues. Fifty-five percent of the communication both ways will happen through nonverbal body language, 38 percent through the tone of what's said, and 7 percent through the actual words. Watch for clues to make sure you're on track.

3. Interviewers are more likely to hire if they have the feeling that you understand *them* and *their problem*.

4. Don't assume that interviewers always know what they're looking for. They may be shopping! Clarify your position and expectations.

5. Make sure you have a purpose going in and a plan of action coming out.

Supportive Follow-up

An interview can be lost in the follow-up. Follow-up is absolutely crucial, yet hardly anybody does it. We often assume that after the interview, we should sit back and wait. Remember, employers offer jobs based on *abilities you communicate to them*. After the interview, you should have enough information to really focus your efforts. Ask yourself: *"What value added can I offer to assist the interviewer in making the decision?"*

Send a thank-you note immediately, that day. Not a typical note, but a *focused* one—review your interview discussion, state any significant insights you gained, reaffirm your interest in the position, inquire about follow-up procedures, and confirm when you expect to hear results or about the next step.

If you really focused, you might also consider sending a functional proposal as follow-up. Such a proposal might consist of the following elements:

1. Cover letter
   a) Review your interview discussion.
   b) State crisply the purpose of this proposal.

2. Background
   a) Describe the situation as the interviewer saw it.
   b) Highlight the specific problem you're most interested in applying your skills and abilities to help solve.

3. Proposal
   a) State your solution or what you would propose to solve the problem.
   b) Embellish your proposal with past accomplishments and/or specific illustrations.

4. Why you?
   a) Briefly review your qualifications.
   b) Refer to and/or attach your functional brief.

5. Benefits to the organization
   a) Project potential benefits to the organization from hiring you and your solution.
   b) Cost to the organization—compare the potential benefits against the salary you would expect.

The focus process is designed to help you put yourself in that successful 10 percent of the population that knows what to look for, knows how to go about the active job search, and does so in a systematic manner. The results are startling! Almost everyone in that 10 percent gets a surge, a glow, a tingle, at the idea of uncovering options. Often these people get job offers in the information-gathering stages because they are efficient and impressive with their self-organization skills. The world does indeed stand aside for a person with a plan!

Let's follow a person through the process and watch it unfold.

Peter decided that resort management (the hospitality industry) offered the greatest prospect for his skills and interests and the kind of life he was looking for. His preliminary reading in the library confirmed that thought. The next question was where? He looked around, wrote for brochures from those ski resorts in areas that most interested him, and settled on several that appeared to suit his needs—about one hundred rooms, four seasons, accommodating winter snow sports and summer water sports, and near a major city.

Next he visited several resorts in northern Minnesota to look at their facilities and activities. He even registered for three days at one to get a good idea of what was going on. At every possible opportunity, he talked with the employees, probed operations behind the scenes, and listened to what guests and employees were saying. It appeared to Peter that well-run Pine Inn was the kind of organization that might have a spot for him.

When Peter had a pretty good appreciation of what was going on, he showed up at the manager's office. At his first attempt, the secretary said, "Mr. Johnson, if you are looking for employment, we don't have any openings." His immediate response was to say, "I have taken some time to study several aspects of the Pine Inn, and I think that the manager would enjoy hearing about some of the problems I have uncovered." Finally getting in to see the manager, Peter expressed strong interest in his operation and appreciation for the good results the manager had achieved.

As the manager warmed to Peter's strong interest in his operation, Peter asked him what the heaviest headaches are that face people in his position and briefly mentioned some of the problems he observed, along with some of his ideas for handling them. During the discussion, Peter discovered areas of real concern to the manager in which he felt he could make a positive contribution. As he did, Peter casually and indirectly touched on his own abilities, attitudes, and experience that would make him an outstanding employee in that kind of operation.

In the context of the focus discussion, Peter's lack of direct experience in resort operations became unimportant to the manager. There simply was no way for the manager to take on new people right then but he gave Peter the names of others in his field whom he should seek. The next day, Peter delivered a copy of a functional proposal to the manager. In his covering note he thanked him for his great help and asked him to let him know if he heard of any opening in the area that he should know about. He offered to work for the manager for one week free of charge. If the manager liked his work, he could hire him on a trial basis. If not, nothing would be lost on either side.

Peter got the job! He's still at Pine Inn, now as assistant manager.

Do It!

23

You have just completed what could be the most important process in your life. You may have discovered skills you never before knew you had, reviewed your life in a new way, felt the ups and the downs of the change process, formed new inventure networks or rejuvenated old ones, set out new goals and planned concrete ways to meet them, made a decision to stay at your present lifestyle or job and put more energy into it. Whatever you've concluded at the end of the process, you are among the people who are on their way to becoming inventurers.

Here's something for you to think about. It was written by an eighty-five-year-old inventurer, and it speaks for itself.

PICKING DAISIES
If I had my life to live all over again, I would pick more Daisies.
If I had my life to live over, I would try to make more mistakes next time,
I would be sillier than I have been this trip,
I would relax. I would limber up.

I know very few things I would take seriously. I would be crazier,
I would be less hygenic; I would take more chances;
I would take more trips, I would climb more mountains,
swim more rivers, and watch more sunsets.
I would burn more gasoline. I would eat more ice cream and less beans.

I would have more actual troubles, and fewer imaginary ones.
You see, I am one of those people who lives prophylactically
and sensibly and sanely, hour after hour, day after day.

Oh, I have had my mad moments, and if I had it to do all over again,
I would have more of them; in fact, I'd try to have nothing else,
just moments, one after another, instead of living so many years ahead.
I have been one of those people who never go anywhere without a thermometer,
a hot-water bottle, a gargle, a raincoat and a parachute.
If I had it to live all over again I would go places and travel lighter than I have.
If I had my life to live over again, I would start barefoot earlier in the spring,
and stay that way later in the fall. I would play hookey more,
*I would ride on more merry-go-rounds. I'd pick more Daisies.**

We urge you to make a decision at some point in your life (preferably now) that you believe in yourself, your skills, your lifestyle options, and your interests and that life means juggling all those factors in different ways for continual renewal. It never stops—even if you try to make it stop.

Make a decision to join the other folks who are becoming inventurers—join the club.

Inventurers are people who are taking charge and creating their own challenges to get themselves moving. More specifically, you are an inventurer if you are willing to take a long look at yourself and consider new options, venture inward, and explore. You are an inventurer if you see life as a series of changes, changes as growth experiences, and growth as positive. You are inventuring on life's *excursions* and learning about yourself as a result. You are willing to risk some disappointments in your quest because you are committed to a balanced lifestyle and to more than just making a living. You are part of a unique group of people who want to make a living work. If you have these qualities, you are an inventurer.

Make a decision. We encourage you, we challenge you, we dare you. And when you do, let us know what it is so we can share with other people your successes (see p. 65).

Make a decision that your life is too short to let yourself be stopped by waiting, by postponement games, by ruts. Recognize the fact that you could cage yourself up indefinitely unless you act. There are four elements that each inventurer must keep in mind for life and career renewal success. With these you can get out of the CAGES you are in. And with these four elements we will close this book.

---

*Summarized by permission from Nathaniel Lande, *Mindstyles/Lifestyles*, Los Angeles: Price/Stern/Sloan, 1976, p. 234.

C Choices and options

A Aloneness

G Guts, courage

E Energy

S Support

Be an inventurer!

Name

Address (optional)

The following progress has been made six months to one year after completion of *The Inventurers*.

1. *Current lifestyle/career*—I have:

    _____ reviewed my lifestyle and am satisfied, happy.

    _____ reviewed my lifestyle and am making changes.

    _____ completed my career-growth proposal and met with my supervisor or mentor.

    _____ made changes in my current job.

    _____ reviewed my job and am satisfied.

    _____ decided that it's too early to predict what will happen.

2. *Future options:*

    _____ I am exploring lifestyle changes.

    _____ I am exploring career changes.

    _____ I have changed jobs.

    _____ I have changed careers.

Share your inventure story with us and send to: Janet Hagberg and Dick Leider, c/o General Books, Addison-Wesley Publishing Company, Reading, Massachusetts 01867.

Appendixes

The Excursion-Skills Checklist

A

OPTION 2: EXCURSION-MEMO EXERCISE

The excursion memo is a device for approaching and using the skills checklist (p. 110) in a more systematic way. Very simply, it is a memo written to you, from you. The memo describes some achievement, peak experience, key event, period of time, job, work situation, or project which you feel good about. It is one to five pages in length (depending on your style) and is written very simply. It describes what you did or accomplished, how you did it, with whom, at what odds, with what resources, for what reward, and how it affected you. For best results, write three excursion memos derived from work or volunteer experiences (including current job) and two memos derived from nonwork (hobby, travel, family, church, etc.) experiences. Divide your paper by drawing a line down the center and writing on the left side.

EXCURSION MEMO

Experience   *Skills*

Experience   *Skills*

Experience   *Skills*

Experience   *Skills*

When you finish the memos, read at least two of them to one or more members of your inventure network. After peeking at the skills checklist, they will help you pick out root and survival skills that they hear you discussing, or they will pick out skills you had to have in order to accomplish what you did, even if you didn't mention them. Write them in the skills column on your memo. One general rule: *Do not put yourself down by negating or denying or minimizing skills.* There are enough people who tell you what you can't do. This is a time to elaborate on what you *can* do. Brag a little. In fact, brag a lot!

Now go to the checklist:

- First, enter you memos in the excursion-memo columns on the top of the checklist.

- Second, go through the checklist and check off the skills you were using in your excursion-memo experience. Then compare these checks with the list you and your partner(s) brainstormed. Did any new ones come to mind that did not come up in your initial review?

- Third, go through the checklist again and circle the skills you remember most enjoying at the time you were involved in that excursion-memo experience.

- Fourth, how do these skills compare with your first impression?

- Fifth, do the same for each memo you wrote.

- Sixth, enter your top three skill clusters that appear most frequently on your excursion map (Box 14).

OPTION 3: SKILLS GRAPH

Directions

1. Fill in your interest levels on the skills graph (fig. A.1). Read each area, A–F, on the skills graph. Think of which areas interest you the most, not what you're good at or what you've done at work or your area of expertise. Just look at what you like, what areas you're most interested in.

2. Mark with an "X" on the graph under each area the level that corresponds to your interest. Full moon indicates the highest interest; low, sleepy moon indicates no interest. If you are interested in everything mentioned in area A, for example, you'd put an "X" on the top line. If you are interested only in the "persuading" part of area E, you might mark low moon, 25 percent. It's a relative graph; just reflect an idea of your interests.

3. Now join the "Xs" with a red line; the height of each area of the graph and the overall shape will give you a reading of the range of interest you have. For a few people, everything will be high; for others, most levels will be in the middle. Some will have enormous peaks and valleys.

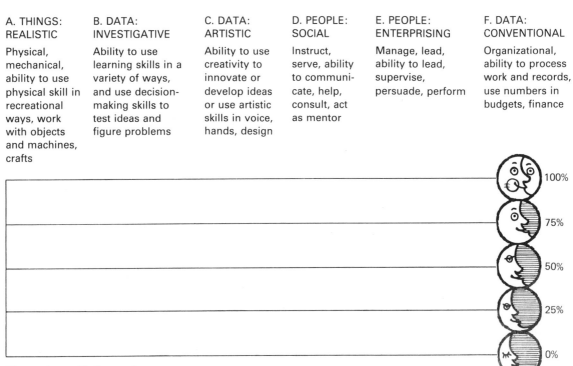

A. THINGS: REALISTIC	B. DATA: INVESTIGATIVE	C. DATA: ARTISTIC	D. PEOPLE: SOCIAL	E. PEOPLE: ENTERPRISING	F. DATA: CONVENTIONAL
Physical, mechanical, ability to use physical skill in recreational ways, work with objects and machines, crafts	Ability to use learning skills in a variety of ways, and use decision-making skills to test ideas and figure problems	Ability to use creativity to innovate or develop ideas or use artistic skills in voice, hands, design	Instruct, serve, ability to communi-cate, help, consult, act as mentor	Manage, lead, ability to lead, supervise, persuade, perform	Organizational, ability to process work and records, use numbers in budgets, finance

Figure A.1. Skills graph.

4. Consider your skill or competence level in each area. After reviewing and completing your checklist, using the excursion memos, mark with an "X" the level you reached in each area and connect the "Xs" with a blue line. Are your skills and interests similar?

5. Let someone who knows you well go through the checklist and pick out skills you do well and those you are best at, in that person's opinion. Go back to the skills graph and mark their levels with "Xs." Connect the "Xs" with a black line.

OPTION 4: SKILLS CHECKLIST (LONG FORM)

Quantity and Quality Scoring Exercise (Fig. A.2)

1. Complete the checklist using the excursion memos and the skills graph.
2. Rate each skill you've checked (whether once or four times) as to the level of competence you achieved (awkward, adequate, competent, very competent).

3. On the Quantity side of the checklist (left side), add the number of checks you made in each column and put the total in the box at the bottom of that column, marked "check totals." Some columns will be longer than others. Add the total of all your columns and place the number in the box marked "average" at the bottom of the Quantity columns.

4. Count the total number of Quantity columns used and put that number in the same Quantity box marked "average." Divide the total by the number of columns to get the average. Write the average in the same box as the totals.

5. Move to the Quality side of the checklist (right side). Add all the numbers together to get a sum total. Put the total in the right-hand box marked "average."

6. Now *count* the number of ratings you gave yourself (not the number of columns used). Divide your sum total by the number of ratings you made, to get an average rating. Write the number of ratings and the average in the "average" box on the right side.

7. Now move to the score section below the boxes. Multiply the average from the left box times ($\times$) the average from the right box to get a total score. Find your total score for each skill group, A through F.

8. Look up your total score on the scoring key to find your relative strength in each skill area. You must be strong in the entire skill group and have high qualitative ratings to rate in the exceptional or outstanding levels.

9. Now go back and eyeball the entire checklist to find the strongest skill areas within the larger groups, e.g., C1 Creative Skills. This skill area may be very strong while the overall Group C may look weaker.

10. Rank your skill *groups* from the scoring sheet and write them below. Also, pick out your three best skill *areas* from the entire checklist and write them below.

My Skill Group Ratings: (e.g., B, Investigative)

Best Skill Group (A–F)	Group _____, _____
Second Skill Group (A–F)	Group _____, _____
Third Skill Group (A–F)	Group _____, _____

My Strongest Skill Areas: (e.g., D, 2, Instruction)

Best Skill Area (A–F, 1–4)	Area _____, _____
Second Skill Area (A–F, 1–4)	Area _____, _____
Third Skill Area (A–F, 1–4)	Area _____, _____

GROUP C—DATA: ARTISTIC

1. Creative Skills

    Imagining, intuiting, predicting
    Innovating, creating new ideas,
      experimenting
    Synthesizing, developing models,
      applying theory

    Perceiving shapes and design

    Other:

2. Artistic Skills

    Sensitivity to beauty

    Using facial expression, voice
    Symboling, visualizing, composing
      (music, poetry, photography)

    Designing visuals, fashions

    Directing productions

    Other:

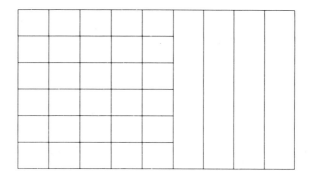

Check Totals   Number Totals

Average =   (total) ÷ (# of columns used)   (sum) ÷ (# rating)   = Average

          Quantity   Quality

SCORE: _____ × _____ = _____

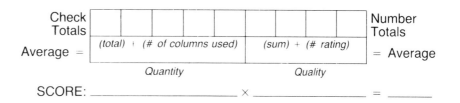

Scoring Key for the Root-Skills Checklist

GROUP A–Things: *Realistic*

0–14	Average skill
15–22	Strong skill
23–29	Exceptional skill
30–44	Outstanding skill

GROUP B–Data: *Investigative*

0–12	Average skill
13–18	Strong skill
19–24	Exceptional skill
25–36	Outstanding skill

GROUP C–Data: *Artistic*

0–12	Average skill
13–18	Strong skill
19–24	Exceptional skill
25–36	Outstanding skill

GROUP D–People: *Social*

0–28	Average skill
29–42	Strong skill
43–56	Exceptional skill
57–84	Outstanding skill

GROUP E–People: *Enterprising*

0–31	Average skill
32–46	Strong skill
47–62	Exceptional skill
63–92	Outstanding skill

GROUP F–Data: *Conventional*

0–12	Average skill
13–18	Strong skill
19–24	Exceptional skill
25–36	Outstanding skill

GROUP A—THINGS: REALISTIC

	QUANTITY RATING				QUALITY RATING			
Overall impression / Most enjoyed	Present job	Excursion memo #1	Excursion memo #2	Excursion memo #3	Awkward (entry) 1	Adequate (skilled) 2	Competent (performance) 3	Very Competent (mastery) 4

1. Physical Skills

   Using coordination and agility
   Outdoor—tennis, running, hiking,
     biking, camping, skiing, fishing
   Indoor—exercising, swimming,
     basketball, racketball, dancing

   Caring for plants, animals, farming

   Traveling, navigating skills

   Other:

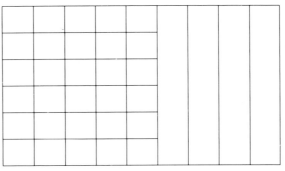

2. Mechanical Skills

   Designing, shaping, composing
     objects and machines
   Setting up equipment, adjusting
     equipment, repairing, controlling
   Assembling, building with precision,
     operating
   Lifting, balancing, moving,
     selecting tools

   Washing, cleaning, tending
   Cooking, crafts (woodworks,
     needlework)

   Other:

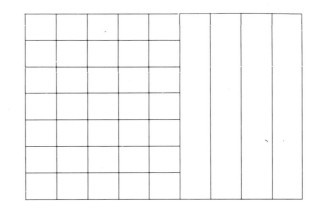

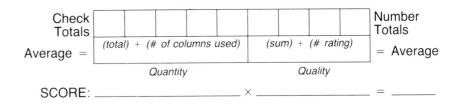

Check Totals | | | | | | | | | Number Totals

Average = (total) ÷ (# of columns used) | (sum) ÷ (# rating) = Average

Quantity | Quality

SCORE: _____ × _____ = _____

GROUP B—DATA: INVESTIGATIVE

1. Learning Skills

   Sensing, feeling, active involvement
   Observing, reflecting, perceptive of
     others
   Reasoning, abstract, using logic,
     data

   Experimenting, piloting, testing

   Estimating, assessing others

   Other:

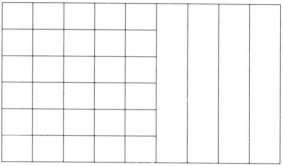

2. Decision-making Skills

   Clarifying problems
   Researching, surveying, analyzing,
     diagnosing problems

   Testing out ideas, troubleshooting
   Reviewing, critiquing, evaluating,
     choosing, inspecting (ideas)

   Other:

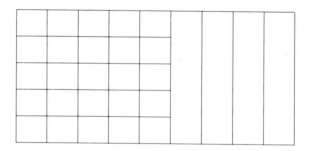

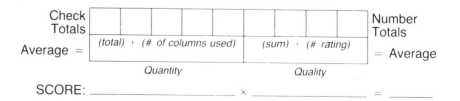

Check Totals / Number Totals

Average = (total) ÷ (# of columns used)   (sum) ÷ (# rating) = Average

Quantity   Quality

SCORE: _____ × _____ = _____

GROUP C—DATA: ARTISTIC

1. Creative Skills

   Imagining, intuiting, predicting
   Innovating, creating new ideas,
     experimenting
   Synthesizing, developing models,
     applying theory

   Perceiving shapes and design

   Other:

2. Artistic Skills

   Sensitivity to beauty

   Using facial expression, voice
   Symboling, visualizing, composing
     (music, poetry, photography)

   Designing visuals, fashions

   Directing productions

   Other:

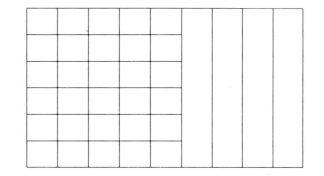

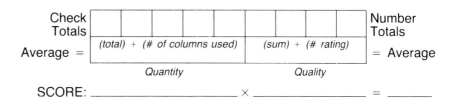

Check Totals   Number Totals

Average = (total) + (# of columns used)   (sum) + (# rating) = Average

Quantity   Quality

SCORE: _____ × _____ = _____

GROUP D—PEOPLE: SOCIAL

1. Communication Skills

   Speaking clearly, effectively

   Writing—reports, letters, memos
   Writing—promotional, creative,
   editing

   Reading—comprehension, speed

   Translating, explaining

   Other:

2. Instruction Skills

   Coaching, informing, leading,
   facilitating groups

   Designing educational materials
   Creating learning environments,
   events
   Illustrating theories and principles
   through examples

   Other:

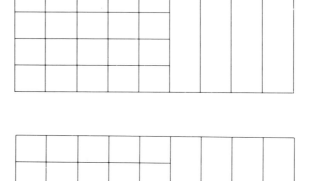

3. Human Relations Skills
   Using counseling skills—empathy,
   rapport, patience, understanding
   Caring for, nursing, soothing
   others
   Managing office activities,
   atmosphere
   Negotiating, representing,
   advocating

   Other:

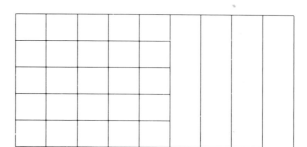

GROUP D—PEOPLE: SOCIAL (Continued)

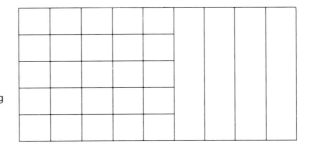

	QUANTITY RATING					QUALITY RATING			
Overall impression ✓ Most enjoyed ⓨ	Present job	Excursion memo #1	Excursion memo #2	Excursion memo #3	Awkward (entry) 1	Adequate (skilled) 2	Competent (performance) 3	Very Competent (mastery) 4	

4. Mentoring Skills

   Listening and questioning others,
     reflecting, guiding, reviewing
   Diagnosing others, evaluating
     feelings, giving feedback
   Developing others, coaching, fore-
     casting, encouraging, motivating
   Sharing responsibility, problem
     solving, team building

   Other:

5. Consulting Skills (used in indirect
   reporting relationships only)

   Giving ideas, clarifying procedures,
     developing rapport
   Informing, advising, assisting,
     guiding, persuading others
   Conferring, diagnosing, discussing,
     resolving, cooperating
   Recommending alternatives, following
     through, evaluating

   Other:

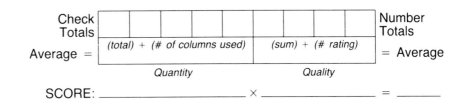

Check Totals   Number Totals

Average =   *(total) + (# of columns used)*   *(sum) + (# rating)*   = Average

                 Quantity   *Quality*

SCORE: _____ × _____ = _____

GROUP E—PEOPLE: ENTERPRISING

						Quantity Rating				Quality Rating		

1. Leadership Skills

   Initiating activities, ideas

   Organizing time, self-direction
   Planning changes, anticipating
     problems

   Solving problems, using alternatives

   Risk taking, inspiring

   Other:

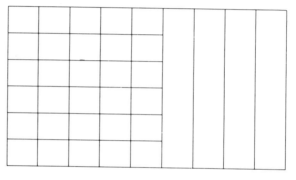

2. Managing/Supervising Skills
   Setting goals and standards,
     assigning tasks

   Organizing others, coordinating
   Planning, developing, organizing
     ideas
   Designing projects, procedures,
     timetables
   Evaluating progress, choosing
     alternatives, troubleshooting
   Implementing policies, responsi-
     bilities
   Evaluating performance of
     individuals

   Other:

GROUP E—PEOPLE: ENTERPRISING (Continued)

	QUANTITY RATING				QUALITY RATING			
Overall impression ✓ / Most enjoyed ⊘ / Present job	Excursion memo #1	Excursion memo #2	Excursion memo #3	Awkward (entry) 1	Adequate (skilled) 2	Competent (performance) 3	Very Competent (mastery) 4	

3. Persuading Skills

   Influencing others, selling

   Developing trust, rapport

   Motivating others, coaxing
   Developing arguments, plotting,
     choosing strategy
   Managing conflict, reconciling,
     arbitrating

   Flexibility, stamina, follow through

   Other:

4. Performing Skills
   Performing, acting, using humor,
     spontaneity

   Modeling
   Public speaking, reading, telling
     stories

   Playing music, singing, dancing

   Competing at sports, games

   Other:

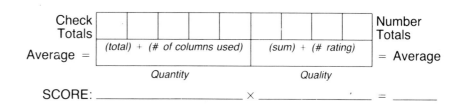

Check Totals   Number Totals

Average = (total) ÷ (# of columns used) | (sum) ÷ (# rating) = Average

Quantity   Quality

SCORE: _____ × _____ = _____

GROUP F—DATA: CONVENTIONAL

1. Detail Skills

   Keeping deadlines, details, accuracy

   Accepting responsibility, executing
   Making contacts, arrangements,
     brokering
   Organizing records, classifying,
     filing, processing

   Clerical skills, office machines

   Other:

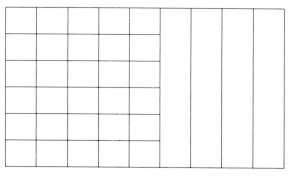

2. Numerical Skills

   Inventorying, classifying
   Using computational, statistical
     abilities
   Financial record keeping,
     appraising, projecting
   Managing budgets, money,
     allocating resources

   Other:

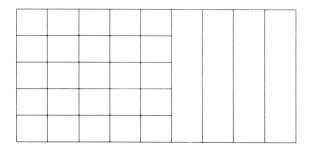

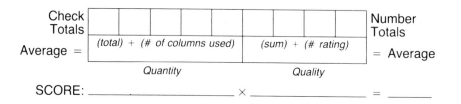

Check Totals   Number Totals

Average = (total) + (# of columns used) | (sum) + (# rating) = Average

            Quantity   Quality

SCORE: _____ × _____ = _____

Nine-Dots
Exercise

B

The solution to the nine-dots exercise is as follows:

Of course, most people see the nine dots as a square and are careful not to go outside the box in connecting the dots. Unless you drew outside the nine dots, you couldn't successfully complete the puzzle.

A major problem for people considering life or career renewal is that they have a hard time getting outside the nine dots—the regular routines, the things they've always done. They are afraid to think creatively. In the brainstorming exercises that follow the nine-dots example, push yourself to expand your ideas and to dream wildly. You'll get a chance later to test out reality. Unless you dream, you'll never get to the first step.

Bibliography

Alberti, Dr. R. E., and Dr. Michaell Emmons, *Your Perfect Right*, San Louis Obispo, California: Impact, 1970.

American Friends Service Committee, *Working Loose*, San Francisco: 1971.

Baldwin, Christina, *One to One: Self-Understanding through Journal Writing*, New York: M. Evans, 1977.

Baldwin, Roger, et. al., *Expanding Faculty Options*, Washington: D.C.: American Association of Higher Education, 1981.

Becker, Ernest, *The Denial of Death*, New York: Free Press, 1973.

Bennett, Hal, and Mike Samuels, *The Well Body Book*, New York: Random House/Bookworks, 1973.

Benson, Herbert, *The Relaxation Response*, New York: Avon, 1976.

Biggs, Don, *Breaking Out*, New York: David McKay, 1973.

Bolles, Richard, *The Quick Job Hunting Map*, Berkeley, California: Ten Speed Press, 1975.

———, *What Color Is Your Parachute?* Berkeley, California: Ten Speed Press, 1974.

Browne, Harry, *How I Found Freedom in an Unfree World*, New York: Avon, 1973.

Byrd, Richard, *A Guide to Personal Risk Taking*, New York: AMACOM, 1974.

Campbell, David P., *If You Don't Know Where You're Going, You'll Probably End Up Somewhere Else*, Niles, Illinois: Argus, 1974.

Crystal, John, and Richard Bolles, *Where Do I Go from Here with My Life?* New York: Seabury Press, 1974.

Dass, Ram, *Grist for the Mill*, Santa Cruz, California: Unity Press, 1977.

———, *The Only Dance There Is*, Santa Cruz, California: Unity Press, 1974.

Drucker, Peter, *Management: Tasks, Responsibilities, Practices*, New York: Harper & Row, 1974.

Edwards, Betty, *Drawing on the Right Side of the Brain*, Los Angeles: Tarcher, Inc., 1979.

Erickson, Erik, *Life History and the Historical Moment*, New York: Norton, 1975.

Ferguson, Marilyn, *The Aquarian Conspiracy*, Los Angeles: Tarcher, Inc., 1980.

Figler, Howard, *The Complete Guide to Job Hunting*.

Frankl, Viktor E., *Man's Search for Meaning*, New York: Washington Square Press, 1963.

Fried, Barbara, *The Middle Age Crisis*, New York: Harper & Row, 1976.

Friedman, M., and R. H. Rosenman, *Type A Behavior and Your Heart*, New York: Knopf, 1974.

Furniss, W. Todd, *Reshaping Faculty Careers*, Washington, D.C.: American Council on Education, 1981.

Gardner, John W., *Excellence*, New York: Harper & Row, 1961.

———, *Self-Renewal*, New York: Harper & Row, 1964.

Glasser, William, *Positive Addiction*, New York: Harper & Row, 1976.

Goodman, Ellen, *Turning Points*, Garden City, New York: Doubleday, 1979.

Gould, Roger, *Transformations*, New York: Simon and Schuster, 1978.

Greco, Ben, *New Careers for Teachers*, Homewood, Illinois: Dow Jones-Irwin, 1976.

Haldane, Bernard, *Career Satisfaction and Success: A Guide to Job Freedom*, New York: AMACOM, 1974.

Hall, Douglas, *Careers in Organizations*, Pacific Palisades, California: Goodyear, 1976.

Heilbrun, Carolyn, *Reinventing Womanhood*, New York: W.W. Norton & Co., 1979.

Herzberg, Frederick, *Work and the Nature of Man*, Cleveland: World, 1966.

Hesse, Herman, *Siddartha*, New York: New Directions, 1951.

Holland, John L., *Making Vocational Choices—A Theory of Careers*, New York: Prentice-Hall, 1973.

———, *The Self-Directed Search*, Palo Alto, California: Consulting Psychologists Press, 1970.

Hunsaker, Phillip L., Douglas J. Mickelson, and Len Sperry, *You Can Make It Happen*, Reading, Massachusetts: Addison-Wesley, 1977.

Irish, Richard, *Go Hire Yourself an Employer*, New York: Anchor Press, 1973.

————, *If Things Don't Improve Soon I May Ask You to Fire Me*, New York: Anchor Books/Doubleday, 1976.

Johnson, Wendell, *People in Quandaries*, New York: Harper & Bros., 1946.

Jourard, Sidney, *The Transparent Self*, New York: D. Van Nostrand, 1964.

Jung, C.G., *Man and His Symbols*, Garden City, New York: Doubleday, 1964.

Kazantzakis, Nikos, *Zorba the Greek*, New York: Simon & Schuster, 1952.

Keen, Sam, *What to Do When You're Bored and Blue*, Wideview Books, 1980.

Kellogg, Marion S., *Career Management*, New York: AMACOM, 1972.

Kirby, Patricia, *Cognitive Style, Learning Style, and Transfer Skill Acquisition*, Columbus, Ohio: Ohio State University, National Center for Research in Vocational Education, 1979.

Knowles, Malcolm, *The Adult Learner: A Neglected Species.* Houston: Gulf, 1973.

Kolb, David, "Learning Style Inventory Technical Manual," Boston: McBer and Co., 1976.

————, "The Experiential Learning Theory of Career Development," in *New Perspectives on Organizational Careers*, ed. J. Van Mannen, New York: Wiley, 1976.

Lakein, Alan, *How to Get Control of Your Time and Your Life*, New York: Wyden, 1973.

Lande, Nathaniel, *Mindstyles/Lifestyles*, Los Angeles: Price/Stern/Sloan, 1976.

Lathrop, Richard, *Who's Hiring Who*, Reston, Virginia: Reston, 1976.

Leider, Richard, and James Harding, *Taking Stock: A Daily Self-Management Journal*, Portland, Oregon: Leider-Harding Publishing Company, 1981.

LeShan, E. J., *The Wonderful Crisis of Middle Age*, New York: David McKay, 1973.

Levinson, D. J., *Seasons of a Man's Life*, New York: Ballantine, 1978.

Livesey, Herbert B., *Second Chance: Blueprints for Life Change*, Philadelphia: J. B. Lippincott, 1977.

Maitland, David, *Against the Grain*, New York: Pilgrim Press, 1981.

Maslow, Abraham, *Toward a Psychology of Being*, New York: D. Van Nostrand, 1961.

Moody, Raymond, *Life After Life*, Harrisburg, Pennsylvania: Stackpole, 1976.

Moustakas, Clark, *Loneliness*, Englewood Cliffs, New Jersey: Prentice-Hall, 1961.

Myers, Isabel Briggs, *Gifts Differing*, Palo Alto, California: Consulting Psychologists Press, Inc., 1980.

Newman, James W., *Release Your Brakes!* New York: CBS, 1977.

Nickles, Elizabeth, *The Coming Matriarchy*, New York: Seaview Books, 1981.

Niehardt, John G., *Black Elk Speaks*, New York: Pocket Books, 1972.

Olson, Sigurd, *Reflections from the North Country*, New York: Knopf, 1976.

Olson, Tillie, *Silences*, New York: Dell Publishing Company, 1965.

O'Neill, Nena, and George O'Neill, *Shifting Gears*, New York: M. Evans, 1974.

Ornstein, Robert E., *The Psychology of Consciousness*, New York: Viking, 1972.

Paulus, T., *Hope for the Flowers*, New York: Paulist Press, 1972.

Pearse, R. R., and B. P. Pelzer, *Self-Directed Change for the Mid-Career Manager*, New York: AMACOM, 1975.

Pelletier, Kenneth, *Mind as Healer, Mind as Slayer*, New York: Dell Publishing Company, 1977.

Phifer, Keith R., *Whole in One*, Osseo, Minnesota: Key Ray Publishing, 1977.

Pirsig, Robert, *Zen and the Art of Motorcycle Maintenance*, New York: Bantam, 1974.

Robbins, Paula, *Successful Midlife Career Change*, New York: AMACOM, 1978.

Russell, Bertrand, *In Praise of Idleness*, New York: Simon & Schuster,

———, *The Conquest of Happiness*, London: Unwin, 1975.

Samples, R., *The Metaphoric Mind*, Reading, Massachusetts: Addison-Wesley, 1977.

Sangiuliano, Iris, *In Her Time*, New York: Morrow Quill, 1980.

Scarf, Maggie, *Unfinished Business*, Briarcliff Manor, N.Y.: Stein & Day, 1972.

Schaef, Anne Wilson, *Women's Reality*, Minneapolis: Winston Press, 1981.

Scholz, Nelle, Judith Prince, and Gordon Miller, *How to Decide: A Guide for Women*, New York: College Entrance Examination Board, 1975.

Schumacher, E. F., *Small Is Beautiful*, New York: Harper & Row, 1975.

Selye, Hans, *Stress Without Distress*, Philadelphia: J. B. Lippincott, 1974.

———, *The Stress of Life*, New York: McGraw-Hill, 1950.

Sheehy, Gail, *Passages*, New York: E. P. Dutton, 1976.

———, *Pathfinders*, New York: William Morrow and Co., 1981.

Spradley, James, and Robert Veninga, *The Work Stress Connection*, Boston: Little, Brown and Co., 1981.

Storey, Walter, *Career Dimensions I–IV*, New York: General Electric Co., 1976.

Terkel, Studs, *Working*, New York: Pantheon, 1972.

Tsu, Lao, *The Way of Life*, New York: New American Library, 1959.

Weaver, Peter, *You, Inc*, New York: Doubleday, 1973.

Zunin, Leonard, and Natalie Zunin, *Contact: The First Four Minutes*, New York: Ballantine, 1972.